DADDY
WAS AN
EXORCIST

Blessing Macho

To Planet Fitness girls,
Hope this true story of mine
inspires and blesses you

Blessing

Macho, Blessing
Daddy Was An Exorcist

Paperback, First Edition

Memoir

Printed in the United States of America

Patrick L. Macho

Blessing Macho

PROLOGUE

This book is a collection of childhood memories of my religious upbringing. I experienced it through a child's perspective, with all of a child's limited understanding; but as an adult, this is how I now remember it:

Dad liked to use the Bible to make decisions. He would open the Bible to a random page and put his finger down on a passage, believing that God would speak to him through whatever verse was selected. He believed the Bible could be relied on for any decision he had to make: where to live, what to name his children.

When I was born, he opened the Bible to Psalms, and the word *blessing* was printed multiple times on the page. I was named Blessing. I was not given a middle name. Dad was afraid that if he gave me a middle name, people might call me by that name rather than Blessing, so he prevented it. My full name is Blessing Macho. The last two children born after me got similar biblical names also: Jon for John the Baptist in the New Testament and Rebekah for Rebekah and Ruth in the Old Testament.

I was born into a family of five children. Jess was the oldest; he was eleven when I was born. He was followed by my sister Conny, brother Gregg, and twin sisters Lynne and Lilly. They were the all-American, blonde-haired, blue-eyed children, and they were born into, what should have been, the perfect family. Dad had a good job, Mom was the faithful housewife, and they lived in a great house.

Six years after the twins were born, I came along. By then, everyone thought Dad had gone a little crazy. Somewhere between the Norman Rockwell existence and my birth, Dad submerged himself in religion.

Dad believed God told him to give up his worldly possessions and follow Him, just like the disciples did in the Bible. So, Dad gave everything away and quit his job to follow the Lord. He sold the beautiful house he had built by hand in the upscale subdivision and moved the family into a smaller house that was in a poor neighborhood in the middle of the city.

Dad had a garage sale to get rid of everything, including the expensive TV that had been recently purchased. Everything was to be sold except the bare essentials. Then, he believed the Lord had given him a new inspiration: give all of the money from the garage sale away, so he sent all of the proceeds to an orphanage in Mexico.

Our new house was called the Coffee House. This was the meeting place for the new church Dad helped to start. The church was called Streams of Life. It eventually grew and became a large congregation. Dad held prayer meetings with the other elders and began preaching daily. People came off the streets to stay in the house — strangers sleeping in our basement.

Some of the people had just gotten out of jail and had nowhere to go. There were some who *had demons* and some who needed to be *saved*. My oldest sister, Conny, later told me of an incident in which Dad had tucked her into bed, and one of the just-released jail birds came upstairs to say goodnight to her. He patted her inappropriately on the bottom and proceeded to do this a couple of times.

This made Conny feel dirty and uncomfortable, so she told Dad. Dad put a stop to it by telling the person he had to leave our home.

Did Dad realize that he had put us kids into harm's way? Danger seemed to follow us as a result of the things he did in our Coffee House home. He began laying hands on people and casting out their demons. And just like that, the normal family life was gone.

It was during this time that I was born.

I was very young when Dad was kicked out of the church he started. The demonology he was involved in and the casting out of demons he performed was too much for the other church elders. They told him he needed to stop casting out demons and performing any type of exorcisms. Dad refused. He did things the way he wanted. The elders gave Dad an ultimatum: stop the exorcisms or leave the congregation. So Dad left and started his own church.

Dad continued casting out demons for a while. There was one woman, in particular, who stayed at our house. Dad said she had the devil inside of her. It got to where she was frightening to us kids.

Conny believed she saw the woman's head turn all the way around once, and she heard the woman speak like a man and make strange animal noises. I remember the numerous pillows strewn all over the house. I thought to myself, how strange, and wondered if this was a game or something.

When I asked Dad, he quickly said no. He had a piercing look in his eyes and his face was beet red. He pointed to the door and bellowed for me to go outside and play. This happened a lot when he did not want me to know what was really happening. I swiftly did as I was told, not wanting to agitate Dad any more than he already was.

Apparently, the reason for the pillows on the stairs was because the possessed woman would try to kill herself by flinging herself over the banister or down the steps. She even tried to throw herself down the laundry chute; she was so petite and slim that the chute could have easily injured her. The woman would have fits, picking up anything and throwing it. It got to be so out of control and dangerous that we kids had to go to the neighbor's house for refuge.

One night in particular, an Elder named Ben, one of a few that stayed in Dad's religious group, was visiting our home. All of a sudden, he heard a loud banging sound followed by cursing. Not wanting to awaken us, since it was late, he took out his harmonica and went up to the woman's room to play it, hoping she would quiet down.

When he opened her door, she leaped onto him, attacking him, trying to choke him. It took all the strength of my Dad and a couple of other elders who were present to get her off of Ben who had deep bite and claw marks from her attack.

Ben did not attend to his bloody, gaping wounds, but instead, he stayed and prayed over the woman. Later, Ben was stunned to see that he did not have one scratch on his body. He was amazed, and he marveled at God's power over the demon.

The other kids and I were awakened by all the commotion, and being so little, we just cried. Ben later told me of the incident and how close we had been to danger.

There was another bizarre occurrence that happened one afternoon at the Agape House next door. It was a scorching afternoon, and I was outside playing with the neighbor kids. Elder John was sitting on the porch and later told me of the strange proceedings inside of the house:

Elder John was sitting quietly, reading the Bible on the front porch swing, when another elder shoved open the front door and shakily gasped, "Did someone call the cops?"

John told him no, that he had simply been sitting and reading and did not know of any such thing. So the other elder began telling him what had just happened upstairs where the windows were wide open because of the sweltering heat.

One of the other elders had come under attack by a demon spirit and started cursing and throwing things, breaking objects against the walls upstairs. It took Dad and a couple of men to hold him down and pray over him. It was so noisy, Dad was concerned a neighbor might have called the cops because of the earsplitting outbursts from the demon spirit.

I had heard nothing and was surprised by the door being flung open so quickly and Dad looking so perplexed with sweat pouring down his brow. John shook his head, puzzled by what he had just been told. It seemed extraordinary and incomprehensible that the event had just happened, and we did not hear it.

For a while, Dad backed off of the demonology a bit.

One

A few years after I was born, my brother
Jon came along. It was during this time that I
started having horrific dreams, nightmares that
woke me up in a shaking sweat, scaring me so
much that I called out for Dad. In my dream, I
remember being all alone in a desert, lost with
no food or water and no one to find me. It was
so real to me, and the same dream happened
repeatedly.

Each time I had the dream, I would wake
up and call to Dad. He would come into my
room, sit on the edge of my bed and say a
prayer with me. He helped me to relax and
would stay with me until I went back to sleep.
Every nightmare from then on, he patiently
stayed at my bedside until I fell asleep. I do not
know if Dad helped the other kids when they
had a bad dream, but he helped me. I felt closer
to Dad because of it, as if I were Daddy's special
girl.

It was getting to be a full house, and
Rebekah was not even born yet. (She would
come a few years later when I was seven, and
she would be the last of the Macho clan.) Space
was tight, and Jess eagerly offered to move into
the attic. Dad had some carpentry skills, so he

bought lumber and hardware, and he turned our attic into a fifth bedroom.

It was cramped, but for Jess, it was a private paradise. It was his own secluded refuge where he could listen to rock and roll music to his heart's delight. That kind of music was forbidden by Dad in our house of God. Sometimes Jess would turn the music up loud, and our father would get angry. Then I would hear Dad march up the stairs and tell Jess to turn it off. But Jess would turn it on again as soon as Dad left, only not so loud.

Sometimes, I snuck up the creaky stairs to the attic and spied on big brother Jess, whom I rarely saw around the house. He always heard me because of the squeaky stairs. He would tell me to come in and be quiet, because he did not want Dad to hear us. If I was caught in the attic, we both got into trouble.

I glanced over the flashy posters on the walls while heavy-metal music played, and I eyed the shiny miniature muscle cars on the shelf, which Jess told me not to touch. I told him how cool I thought his room was and wished I had more time to visit, but Mom's voice calling me from downstairs stopped me fast.

Jess would say, "Goodbye, and don't tell Dad I let you in my room, okay?" I would answer, "Don't worry, I won't," as I raced down the squeaky stairs to Mom calling me in the kitchen.

None of us children wanted to upset Dad,

because being in trouble was no laughing matter. Dad had a flaming temper. When he shouted, I wanted to run and hide in the closet. It added to our stress level, which was already too high. If we got into trouble, Dad would either spank us or send us to our room to read the Bible. We were often grounded too.

Jess did not stay in the attic for long. He had a newspaper delivery route and was making decent money. Younger brother Gregg offered to help him, since Jess had become quite busy. Pretty soon, they teamed up with the local newspaper and were making some serious and much needed money. This disappointed my Dad. I think he felt inadequate, and he reiterated that money was the root of all evil.

Dad noticed the older kids acting more ungodly as they became teenagers. Every morning before school, all of us kids had to read the Bible, and we had a prayer meeting after school. Dad said this was to cleanse our minds from the impure things we were learning at public school.

The older kids resented wasting their free time with these prayer sessions. I did not really understand why. Being young, I thought it was fun: sitting together, reading the Bible, singing hymns as one big, happy family. We also sang a Christian song and said grace before our evening meals.

Oldest brother Jess, who hardly ever seemed to be home because of his job and school, was becoming too worldly for Dad. He was given the choice to pay rent or move out. He moved out.

I missed him when he left. I was just getting used to sneaking up to his room to visit him when no one was watching, which was rare but loads of fun. I think the new-found religious lifestyle was hardest on him. He was the oldest, and he remembered the *normal life* that was now gone. Being allowed to go trick-or-treating at Halloween and having lots of neighbor friends, whether Christian or not, were some of the fond memories he had.

He was seventeen when he left. He moved out of the Coffee House and into a modern house, gladly paying top dollar to have his own place.

My oldest sister, Conny, moved out soon after Jess. She had a job at a fast food restaurant. She was a cheerleader and had a Trans Am. She was popular and had a lot of friends, and she was not around much. Dad told her she was not obeying God's rules, but she did not think she was doing anything terribly wrong. She argued that her grades were straight A's, and she only had the job to pay for the sports car. She said, "Jesus, what's wrong with a little freedom anyway?"

Dad loathed anybody using the Lord's name in vain. He suggested that she consider leaving if she wanted to live that kind of lifestyle. Conny tried sympathizing with Mom.

She pleaded with Mom to talk to Dad so that she could stay, but Dad just opened his Bible and stopped listening to them.

Mom usually gave in to Dad when it came to family matters. Dad, being deeply enmeshed in his religious mindset, gave Conny a choice. She either had to quit her job and change her ungodly ways or move out like Jess did. So, she chose to leave, moving into the house Jess was renting.

At the time that Conny moved out, I was still very small, and I had not been given enough time to fully know her, but her leaving made me feel empty and miserable inside, and I did not know why. She seemed so perfect. I could not understand why Dad suggested she leave. I did not see what was so wrong with being popular and getting straight A's in school.

I was confused and did not want to say goodbye to my oldest sister, though I did not actually get to say a formal goodbye. She was packed up and gone before I arrived home from school. Little did I know, years would pass before I could speak to her again.

Two

As younger brother Jon and I played out back in the sandbox and fort, doing kid things, the older siblings were more into their friends, jobs, and stylish clothes. It was hard for me to be close to them because of our age difference. I frequently knocked on the twins' closed door, asking if I could come in and hang out with them. They giggled and said, "No, go play outside with Jon."

Of course, I did as I was told. I was disappointed, and I would daydream about being grown-up so I could chill with my older brothers and sisters. They seemed so cool and sophisticated.

On one sporadic occasion, one of the twins lost an earring and allowed me to come into their room to try and find it, since I was smaller and good at finding little objects. I was excited and eager to be in their room, so I quickly found the lost earring and thought maybe, as a reward, they would let me stay in their room and have some girl time.

"Of course not," was Lilly's reply, motioning for me to leave. I dropped my gaze and went out back to play. I shook it off and went to hang on the swing set, pretending I was a monkey.

It was during one of these instances that I heard a loud buzzing coming out of the end of the swing set. Suddenly, this buzz was fluttering in my now bulging eyes. Mere inches from my face was a huge, waxy looking wasp.

Screaming and nearly crying, I ran to Dad, who was fixing something on the side of the house. He told me to be calm and not move a muscle. I crouched low to the ground as the wasp came swirling close to me and landed inches from my knee. I closed my eyes, not wanting to see it sting me. In that same instant, my Dad had squashed the buzzing insect.

I was amazed at how easily Dad took care of the matter, without getting stung. At that moment, Dad was my hero. I gave him a hug for eliminating the threat. He gladly accepted my cuddle, then he went back to the project he had been working on before I disturbed him.

Sometimes, the neighbor kids next door were outside, and I would climb over the fence and play with them. Gretchen and Jonny were their names. I never really asked permission to play with them, I just snuck over the fence, and when Mom poked her head out the back door to see where I was, I waved and told her I was playing on the swings with Gretchen. She just smiled back and said okay. Mom seemed to be a little more tolerant and accepting of things than Dad.

One day, I was out back playing with Gretchen, and we both noticed a cooler sitting out beside the fence with what looked like soda pop inside of it. Since it was a sweltering afternoon and there were plenty of cold cans in the cooler, we thought no one would mind if we shared one.

Gretchen's Dad was inside snoring at the time and we did not want to bother him. We greedily picked up a red and white Budweiser thinking it was soda and took a big gulp. We gagged, spitting out the beer. "Yuck," I said as Gretchen wrinkled her face in response.

That was my first and last beer. To this day, I cannot stand the stuff. We both shook our heads, not understanding how adults could stand to drink this brew when soda tastes so much better. We poured out the rest of the can and hid the evidence.

I had another peculiar experience with a different neighbor girl who lived directly behind me. She looked a little older and wiser than me. I was out back, trying to make a basket with our basketball and was not having much luck.

When she saw me, she came over and said, "Here, let me show you how to get a good shot at the hoop."

"Okay," I said, rather surprised to see someone close to my age who wanted to play with me. There were not many girls on our street so this was a pleasant gesture, or so I thought.

The neighbor girl made a perfect shot, then she told me her name and asked if I wanted to hang out with her. I said yes and led her into our backyard to show her our kid fort attached to the back of the house. It had an upstairs and a downstairs. Dad had built it a few years back. As we went into the fort, she seemed quiet at first and standoffish, and then asked me if I wanted to try something really cool. I said yes, and she looked around to make sure no one else was watching. Then she shut the fort door and told me to lie down in front of her.

I do not remember if she told me to pull my pants and underwear down, or if I let her do it. All of a sudden, she lay her naked body on top of mine and proceeded to hump me. Minutes felt like hours. At first I thought she was going to hurt me. Her breath was hot and steamy and pressed against my face, and soon her breathing became erratic as she let out a heavy gasp.

Almost as quickly as she had gotten on top of me, she got up, now out of breath, and pulled her pants up and smiled, asking me what I thought.

"Sweet, right?" she said and peered down at me as she buttoned up her blouse.

"Sure," I said back, not wanting to disappoint my new, mature friend. I felt strange and scared inside. I could not understand the odd way my body was feeling. My blood just seemed to be crawling beneath my skin.

The girl told me that this was to be our little secret and not to tell anyone. I was perplexed and assured her that I would keep our experience a secret. I did not understand that what we had done was wrong. I did not know anything about being a lesbian.

It was not until later, as I got older, that I started to understand. After our involvement in the fort, I felt awkward and told her I had to go inside and help Mom with dinner preparations. I was lying but did not want to tell her the truth. I was not sure I wanted her to come over any more or do that *sweet thing*. I did not tell anyone else what had happened. I kept our little secret.

I hurriedly went inside and ran upstairs to wash my hands. I felt dirty and unsure how I was going to face her again, though she was my neighbor. Luckily, a short time later, we moved to a little town called Center Point, and I never saw her again. Little did I know that soon, I would not be seeing my Mom again either.

Three

Our family participated in all-day potlucks. We would load up in our worn-out station wagon and head out to a different believer's home each Sunday for fellowship. People would share dreams or visions they felt God had given to them. Dad would lay his hands on people, especially if someone was ill or had an issue that was worrying them.

I was a little older, at this point, and do not recall Dad doing any more full blown exorcisms. He would conduct less dramatic ceremonies, such as casting out a demonic presence or trying to heal somebody with God's *powerful words* rather than condoning the use of modern medicine. Some people believed the Lord's power was remarkably at my Dad's fingertips, but others were not so sure.

There were times when Dad referred to a demon as simply one of God's creatures so he would not scare the person it presumably inhabited. He labeled them in animal terms, such as: *having a gorilla, serpent, or monkey on your back.* Dad claimed to have a third eye. He said that he could see spiritual things. He told me that it was a gift from God to help others who were not as strong with the Lord.

Usually the service would start with hymns and Christian songs. If someone had a guitar or tambourine or violin, they would play. I sometimes stayed for this part and sang beside my mother who wore her long, country skirt and swayed to the music. I would smile and look up at Mom who glanced down at me and grinned back.

Sometimes, baby Rebekah would stand up and wiggle to the music with Mom close behind her. I always burst out laughing when Rebekah swished her jumper outfit from side to side to the rhythm of the chorus. I enjoyed these rare moments and sometimes wished I could bottle up the unique experience. Everyone seemed to have a glow about them as they belted out the music, as though in a trance.

After the singing, I usually went to the play room or outside where the other children my age were playing and joined in with their activities. Most of the time, we chased the farm cats or kittens around in the barn or tossed stones in the nearby creek.

A couple of girls were my age, and we got along great. Rachael and Hannah were their names. I was occasionally allowed to have sleepovers with them. Since they were Christian, Dad said it was okay. I always looked forward to spending the night with them, since their parents were not as strict as Dad. We often would stay up late into the night, either watching shows on TV that I was not allowed to watch, or we listened to rock music on the radio, which also was forbidden in our home.

Sometimes we played dress up, and I would admire some new outfit that they owned. My clothes were hand-me-downs, plain, not stylish like theirs. Dad told me those clothes were not of God, and I was not allowed to have any fashionable clothes or even crave them, which I did anyway. Hannah told me to try one of her outfits on, just to see how I looked. I did and immediately felt special and guilty all at once, because if Dad found out, he would be mad and put an end to the sleepovers. So we were careful not to tell anyone.

The home meetings were one thing I looked forward to, and the week always went by so slowly. These friends from home meetings were the only real friends that Dad allowed me to have. I looked forward to these meetings for a little bit of freedom with my Christian friends.

When Dad laid his hands on people, he would often speak in tongues. It was supposed to be another language, but it did not make any sense to me and just sounded like gibberish. After his *powerful touch*, these people would look up at Dad and thank him in a peaceful, humble manner. I do not know if their pain or sickness was gone, but they always seemed happy with a bit of a glow about them. It was like they were in a passive trance, their own kind of heavenly realm.

To me, my Dad was just that, my Dad. But to people at these home meetings, he was looked up to and listened to when he spoke. According to him, his voice was God, the Father, speaking words of wisdom through him, and his words were not to be taken lightly but absorbed and believed, as if God were speaking.

Sometimes after the hymn singing, I stayed and listened to Dad to see if I could comprehend or receive a higher wisdom from his words. All that came to me was a rumbling in my tummy telling me I was hungry, and I would fidget in my seat, eager to go play with the other kids outside.

Other times, my eyelids barely stayed open as the preaching words droned on and on. Mom always seemed to understand my bored stares and nodded that it was okay for me to go outside with the other children.

Sometimes Mom and Dad would go to prayer meetings at night, and when they did, Gregg would babysit us. Once in a while, Conny would come back to help, too. We had a lot of fun then, breaking Dad's rules. The rock and roll music would come on almost before my parents were out of the driveway. Gregg would command us to dance, and we would all jump on the couch, twisting and turning, dancing to the tune of "Little Red Corvette."

Since we participated, Gregg felt confident we would not squeal on ourselves, keeping him out of trouble. We did not say a word because we thought we might get to do it again sometime. We had a blast. We also played hide and go seek, and these were rare, exciting, fun times for Jon and me that were not to last.

As each older brother or sister moved out, Dad told them they were not allowed to come back home being worldly and unholy in God's eyes. Sinners. Dad disowned each one shortly after they moved out, and the younger ones were not allowed to talk to or see them again. This saddened and disheartened me as I was growing up, since I greatly missed all five older brothers and sisters. I barely got to know or get close to any of them. Dad said they were "going to hell."

When I turned ten, I felt more grownup for some odd reason, maybe because some of the older siblings were gone. We moved to a small town twenty miles north of Cedar Rapids. That is when things really started to go downhill.

Four

"Hi, what's your name?" A girl stood on the dirt road, smiling at me.

"Blessing," I replied, excited to meet someone already. She looked to be about my age, with short, curly red hair and freckles. I was not used to seeing girls with short hair, and for a moment, I thought she was a boy.

"I'm Shannon," the girl said. "Do you want to play?" And just like that, I had a friend.

I was excited to move to Center Point. I thought it would be a new start. It was 1985, and I was ten years old. Dad wanted to move because he thought the big city, if you could call Cedar Rapids a big city, was getting too worldly. That is the word he used for anything that he considered to be against God's laws. And his definition of worldly was broad, encompassing anything from smoking, drinking, and dancing, to watching commercials. Dad hoped that getting away from the city and moving to the country would get us closer to nature and closer to God.

The house was a big, blue, two-story farmhouse with a shed out back that we used as a chicken coop. It had an acre or two that Mom made into a garden. I hated pulling the weeds, because it was such a chore and usually took all day. The front of the house had a wrap-around porch with a swing on the far end. I decided this was going to be my favorite spot.

Once inside, the wood floor squeaked with each step. The large coat room led into the dining room. To the right was the kitchen, and to the left was a dark-paneled family room with bright shaggy orange carpet. Just past the outdated carpet, a door led to what Dad named his *prayer room*. This was the room where we were not to disturb him because God spoke to him there. He usually kept it closed; he would spend a lot of time in this room during the day. We were to be quiet if we were in the living room playing when he was in the prayer room.

In the dining room corner was a nook area by a steep staircase; this nook was where Rebekah, the youngest, could be found playing most of the time.

Jon and I ran upstairs to see which room we would claim. I was drawn to the room with the bright pink butterfly wallpaper. Jon claimed the room just next to it with blue walls. He hung wooden model planes from the ceiling. He and Dad constructed them when Dad had some free time.

Since my room was the biggest, Rebekah and I were to share it, and the older twins would share the distant front room. Mom and Dad's room was directly beside my room. We all shared a hall bath. Dad added a make-shift laundry chute, similar to the one at our last home. The house looked a lot like the green Coffee House we had just left behind. It was big and old, but it had a much larger yard to play in.

Mom spent a lot of her free afternoon time in her room reading the Bible and taking notes in a journal. I think she would do this when she was in pain or not feeling well. I would often call for her, thinking she was in the kitchen but was surprised to find her quietly studying her Bible up in her bedroom.

When I found her there, she looked tired and startled. She would take me downstairs and find me a chore to do or would give me a snack from the kitchen. I think she was trying to hide her pain and suffering from me, and I did not understand why. If I had known, I probably would have comforted her and said a prayer with her to take away the pain.

The kitchen was similar to the one at our old house. Mom started unpacking pots and pans, humming a hymn as she moved about the kitchen. This was the main room where she spent most of her time: cooking dinner, canning goods from the garden, or baking a sweet smelling desert.

There was a big bay window in the dining room where Mom's massive indoor plants took up every inch of space available. I knew she had a green thumb because every plant she grew blossomed with healthy petals all season long. Sometimes, I would help her water her many indoor and outdoor plants with our well water.

The shed out back was not very big, but Mom and Dad agreed to have chickens now that we were in the country. Jon and I were in charge of feeding them. We eagerly agreed to this, since we got to name and hold the cute little chicks.

I was excited to be in a new place and could not wait to explore my surroundings. The small house next door to ours had a rundown garage which Dad said to stay away from because it looked dangerously close to caving in.

However, the minute Dad was not watching, I snuck over to inspect it and heard a faint meow sound coming out of a crack in the side door. All of a sudden, out leapt a tiny fur-ball of energy, and I reached out to grab the fluffy kitten, but it quickly darted back into the crack in the door.

I looked around to see if anyone was watching, not wanting Dad to see me. With the coast clear, I shimmied my way in through the crack. The door barely budged because in the way were piles of old lawnmower parts and sacks of junk. I spotted the kitten inching away, and I scooped it up with one arm and brushed a cobweb away with the other.

"I think I will call you, Chelsea."

I was not sure if Mom or Dad would let me keep him, but I thought it was worth a try. I would tell them that it would keep mice out of our old farmhouse. I heard other cats and kittens in the garage, but I knew if I stayed too long I would surely get into trouble. I felt my way through the dark mess in the garage, hanging on tight to my new startled kitten, and I wiggled back out of the cracked door, trying to be quiet.

Now there was one more hurdle to climb: asking Dad if I could keep it. Figuring his answer would be no, I went to Mom who told me to ask him anyway. His reply was, "Your Mom is allergic to cats, so we can't have it indoors. However, if you want to feed it out back, and it chooses to hang around, then that's okay."

I was thrilled and asked Mom for scraps to feed it. She sweetly smiled as she handed me some chicken skins. I sat on the back porch, giddy with excitement. We had just moved in and my day was off to a great start with my new kitten friend, Chelsea. He purred and came over to me after licking the bowl clean.

As I petted him, I wondered how hard it would be to make new friends in this country town. I hoped I would make friends here as easily as I had met Shannon. She lived at the end of my street. She was not Christian, by Dad's definition, but it was not the first time I fudged the truth. I desperately wanted a friend, so if I had to tell Dad that Shannon was a Christian, then so be it.

That first summer, I spent a lot of my time with Shannon. We played video games at her house. Super Mario Brothers was the new thing, and we spent countless hours trying to rescue the princess. We walked to the convenience store to buy snacks, played on the rope swing in her backyard, chased the neighborhood cats or played at the park.

The summer that we moved to Center Point, Shannon and I had our first smoking experience, the first and last, that is. We were at the town park, as usual, and it was crowded.

Kids splashed in the wading pool and ran through the sprinklers, but Shannon and I made our way to the forts at the other end of the park. It was hot, and the forts made a cool shelter. A boy's voice greeted us from the dark corner as we entered.

"Hey guys," he said, "want to see something cool?"

Of course, Shannon and I wanted to see something cool.

The boy took a step forward, quitting the shelter of the dark corner. A grey haze followed him, surrounding his head, and something acrid tinged my nostrils. It was smoke. He reached into his pocket and pulled out a cigarette. In his other hand, his thumb flicked a lighter, the flame bursting into view, the cigarette hanging from his lips now glowed red.

"Watch this," he said, sucking deeply and blowing out a puff of white smoke.

He was smoking, and he did look cool — cool enough for me to want to try it.

"It's something all the grown-ups do," the boy continued, taking another long drag then handing the cigarette to Shannon and me.

Shannon went first. She tentatively held the cigarette, balancing it between her two fingers like the boy had. She put it to her lips and inhaled deeply, then she stopped short and started coughing. "I think I did it wrong," she croaked, handing the cigarette to me. I hesitated, staring at the glow of fire.

"What, you're not chicken are you?" the boy asked.

I did not want anyone to think I was a chicken, so I grabbed the cigarette between my thumb and forefinger and brought it to my mouth. I just as quickly ripped the cigarette away from my lips, gagging and spitting to get the taste out of my mouth. It was like the taste of ashes from a fire pit. It made me feel dirty.

"I don't like it," I said. Shannon agreed.

The boy just shrugged and took the cigarette back, flicking the ashes on the ground before putting it back to his lips. I did not understand why adults liked it or why they did it, but there were a lot of things about adults I did not understand then.

The summer was coming to an end, and things were beginning to change. Lynne and Lilly were sixteen. Lilly was not spending much time at home anymore. When we moved to Center Point, her stuff moved with us, but she stayed behind, often sleeping at Jess's place. She had a job and a lot of friends who liked to hangout. She would come home sometimes on the weekends, short stays to grab some of her clothing.

The brief visits almost always ended in an argument with Dad. She was too worldly for his taste and needed to repent of her ways and get back to God. I went to my room during these arguments and listened to them shouting at each other downstairs.

One Sunday in August, Lilly had not come home yet, and it was getting to be suppertime. I came home from playing with Shannon, my stomach rumbling as I ran up the front steps of the porch. I ran into Dad coming out, a bag of clothing bulging precariously in his arms. I recognized Lilly's designer shirts on the top.

"What are you doing?" I asked, watching him set the bag on one of the porch chairs.

"Just get in the house," he replied grimly. "Lilly's not welcome here anymore."

I wanted to ask him why, but I knew better. He told me to get in the house, and I obeyed, not liking the harsh tone of his voice. But I worried for Lilly. I was concerned about what this meant for her, where she would go, where she would stay, what she would do. She was still only sixteen.

I ran up to my room, ignoring the hunger pains in my stomach. I sat on my bed and settled my chin onto my hands on the windowsill. Soon, a red Volkswagen Rabbit came into view, roaring around the corner, the tires swirling up dust from the road. Lilly was home.

I watched her park the car on the road, then open the door and walk across the grass, her hair limp from the humidity, her shorts and blouse damp with sweat. She disappeared from my view, then the yelling started downstairs.

I left the window and fell back onto my bed, staring up at the ceiling. I could hear Dad's raised voice loud and clear, drifting up from the porch. The whole neighborhood could probably hear.

"You're disobeying God and God's way," Dad bellowed. "You're not allowed in this house anymore!"

He went on shouting about my sister being too worldly and not following God. I could not hear Lilly's reply, but I did hear the car door slam a few minutes later. She must have gathered the few bags that contained her possessions that Dad had set on the front porch. The car engine roared to life, and I scooted to the window to watch her leave.

I think she was relieved to go, although the look in her eyes was pure sadness. Nothing was left to say between them. She was sixteen and wanted to be a typical teenager, but being typical did not go along with Dad's rules, so she was gone, just like that, and then there were four of us left.

The next year passed, filled with prayers and Bible study and home meetings. I thought I would miss Lilly, but I did not. She was never around much before, and now that she was gone, it was like she had never been there. I had never witnessed her helping Mom with chores, and when she had been asked to help, I had overheard her complaining that she was too busy.

I did not want any of the older brothers or sisters to move out, that was their choice, and as a kid, I did not understand a teenager's rebellious ways.

Lynne had a steady boyfriend, Pat, whom she spent a lot of time with, and one day in June, she brought him home. Mom had seen Pat before—seen him go into a bar, which was a death sentence for his standing with my parents. When they walked up to the house, Mom and Dad were waiting in the front hall. Dad would not let Pat go any further.

I watched from the stairs when they tried to enter. I thought Pat seemed like a nice guy. He was well-mannered and dressed nice. He called Mom *Ma'am* and Dad *Sir*. He said *please* and *thank you*. But he had gone into a bar, and he was already judged. Nothing he could do would change Mom and Dad's opinion of him.

It was an awkward few moments. The air was thick with tension as Dad practically blocked the way, not letting Pat and Lynne enter the house. Pat went back to the car; I am sure he felt about an inch tall after the glare Dad gave him.

As soon as he was out of earshot, Dad bellowed, "You can't see him anymore." Then he proceeded to tell Lynne about how Mom had witnessed Pat going into a bar.

"He's old enough to drink," Lynne shouted back. "What's the big deal?"

"He's not of God," Dad replied.

I could tell Lynne was hurt—I could see it in her face. She wanted Dad and Mom's approval, and they had not given it. Instead, they told her that if she wanted to continue dating him, then she had to move out. I think they thought she would leave Pat and come back to them. But she did not. She left that day and came back only once to get her stuff.

Lynne moved in with Pat's parents. She came back to visit once and tell Mom and Dad that she was getting married. She wanted to ask Dad to walk her down the aisle. Dad told her he did not think it was right in God's eyes that she marry Pat, and he would not walk her down the aisle or even go to the wedding.

Mom was not allowed to go to the wedding either. I saw her crying in the kitchen, and when she noticed me, she quickly turned and went upstairs and continued to cry in her room. I curiously followed her up and overheard her sobs from the bedroom. I did not understand why she was crying; I was still young then. I sat on my bed and quietly said a prayer to God: *"Please Lord, help me to be a decent Christian, unlike my older brothers and sisters. I want to be obedient and behave so Mom and Dad are pleased and not saddened as they are now. Help me to be a worthy servant in your eyes. Amen."*

There were only three of us left then, and at eleven years old, I was now the oldest child in the house. I had to set a good example for the younger two, and I did not want to disappoint my parents.

It was hard on Mom when Lynne left— they had been very close. Mom had called her *my little helper.* Lynne helped Mom in the kitchen, daily preparing dinner fixings: homemade bread, caramel sweet rolls, even wedding cakes. Mom had been making and selling wedding cakes for extra grocery money when Dad did not have many fix-it jobs in the winter months. Her cakes were so delectable, she had a hard time keeping up with demand for them.

Younger brother Jon and I would sit at the kitchen table, patiently watching and waiting for her to finish frosting the cake so we could lick the frosting out of the bowls and gobble up cake toppings Mom scraped off when she cut the tops off of the sheet cakes. Boy was Mom an excellent cook! The frosted roses she made for the cakes were perfect and made beautiful, towering creations that were so neat, you almost did not want to eat it, just stare at it and take a picture.

Every birthday was special in our house for the birthday boy or girl. Mom always made a toy train cake for Jon or teddy bear cake for me, followed with our very favorite meal, which in my case were tacos.

Mom also made goodies around Christmas time. *Jesus's birthday time* was what Dad called it. Chocolate peanut clusters were one of Dads favorites, along with white covered pretzels. My favorite was the Christmas cookies.

All of us kids got to sit down at the kitchen table and make a huge mess with decorating sprinkles and frosting. Each creative cookie was different than the others, and we usually took some to the neighbors and teachers at school. I had a great time decorating with my brothers and sisters. I think Mom enjoyed watching us make the frosted Christmas cookies, humming as she went about the kitchen, lending a helping hand if we needed more sprinkles or frosting.

Jon and I played Christian Christmas music with our instruments for Mom and Dad after we had taken time to practice, so the music blended smoothly together. I played the violin and Jon played the coronet, a small type of trumpet. Dad wanted all of us kids to learn how to play God's music with an instrument, since he had played the drums as a teen in a small band. Dad thought it was an educational and productive thing to do, to learn notes with an instrument.

I liked the viola, a type of violin, and I easily learned how to play it with lessons, although I did grumble a couple times when the weather was nice outside, and I was stuck inside learning notes to play after school. I played a whole year and made second in a school contest once.

Jon mostly practiced at home, up in his room. I thought he was pretty good, although the music got loud at times, and I would yell for him to be quiet. I usually spoke before thinking, and Dad told me to apologize for yelling and go pray to God in my room. Dad said my yelling was disobedient. I caught myself doing this often, and I quickly apologized, not meaning to hurt Brother Jon's feelings.

Not understanding his quiet, shy, sensitive nature either, I soon began to loathe going to my room to pray to God for forgiveness. I did not see how I was in the wrong all the time, remembering back on how Lynne and Lilly had behaved before they left. Not that that was a bad thing. We were all growing up.

Mom cried about Lynne more than once. I felt emptiness in the pit of my stomach. I liked Lynne a lot, even though at the time, she was closer to her twin, Lilly, than to me. I saw how kind and helpful she was with Mom in the kitchen. I did not like to see Mom sad. I knew Lynne had not intentionally tried to hurt Mom by leaving, but she wanted to be with her new boyfriend, Pat, and Dad forbad their relationship, so Lynne had no choice but to move out, since she was in love with him.

I told myself that I would be a faithful, trusting Christian, and I would not be like the older ones, because I saw how much it hurt Mom. We kids meant everything to Mom. She ate, slept and breathed tending to our every need. We meant the world to her. Later, Mom's oldest sister, Judi, told me that all Mom ever wanted to do when she grew up was to get married and have a big family. She got her wish, but things were far from perfect.

The older kids were disowned by Dad, and we were not allowed to talk to them anymore, but I knew Mom would talk to them sometimes. I heard her on the phone when Dad was not around.

Conny wrote me letters, even though we were not supposed to get them, and once in a while, she would send me a souvenir from a trip. One time, I got a shirt from her. It was hot pink with puffy flamingos on the front. It was very stylish and too worldly for Dad's taste, so I hid it in my bedroom, wearing it when Dad was not around. Mom knew about it and allowed it, but neither of us told Dad.

I think Mom understood that I was missing the older sisters, and this was her way of showing me that it was okay to miss them, because she missed them too. I could see it in her eyes, every time Conny called. They would quietly talk for what seemed like an hour when Dad was not nearby to notice.

I was torn between fulfilling Dad's wish for me to be a good Christian and talking and writing to the older siblings now that they were disowned.

Dad got even stricter after Lynne left. Maybe he thought he needed to, because he believed the older ones were on a bad path. He wanted to make sure we did not follow in their footsteps. I heard him pray out loud in his prayer chair in the living room, saying to God that the older ones were involved in bad things, and they were not a part of the church or Jesus anymore, so he had to be more stern with us.

So, where Dad had been *lenient* with the older kids, he was not with us. He started cracking down on me especially. I was not allowed to sleep over at friends' houses anymore or even hang out. I could not wear makeup, do my hair, or wear any stylish clothes — not that we could afford to buy them anyway.

We were poor, poorer than most people, and I was starting to notice it. We were so poor, I even asked at school if I could take home the extra peanut butter sandwiches from lunch, but a kid saw me do it once, and I felt embarrassed, so I stopped.

Dad did not have a steady job like the one he had had at Rockwell. He was now a *disciple*, like in the New Testament, a carpenter, just as Jesus had been. He did odd jobs, like fixing things for neighbors, and he always said, "God will provide." We scraped by, living hand to mouth.

In the summer, Jon and I went with Dad and helped him paint or replace old carpet. I did enjoy helping at these odd jobs; it was nice to spend quality time with Dad that did not have anything to do with religion, just good hard physical labor.

Jon and I took turns going with Dad, and when we were finished, as a reward, he would stop at the gas station so that we could get a snack. I immediately went for a Little Debbie cake and a Dr. Pepper. Looking back, it was a moment in time I cherished with Dad, but I did not like how little money the jobs paid. We barely got by each year, and we seemed to be getting poorer as time passed.

Mom worked a little, sometimes babysitting, which I did too. I loved it because I got to watch television and movies. I was also old enough to have a paper route; my Mom had one too. Early before daylight, Mom shook me awake, and together we sleepily made our way through the quiet streets on our bikes, delivering newspapers. Some mornings when she shook me awake, I would mumble, "It's too early," pulling the covers over my head. I always got up anyway, because I knew we needed the extra money.

Sometimes I would give some of my earnings to Mom so she could buy groceries or have a special treat for us kids after school. Mostly, I tried to save the money. I saved enough to buy myself a pink bike, so I did not have to be embarrassed riding Mom's old Schwinn. I also bought myself some pink high tops, because I wanted to try and fit in with the other kids.

I was a pre-teen, and I was starting to get interested in fashion, but we could not afford new clothes and wearing stylish clothes was not of God, according to Dad. All of my clothes were hand-me-downs, not the stylish, hip clothes the other kids at school wore.

I also wanted to get my ears pierced, and I asked Dad one day if I could. He told me, "If God wanted your ears to be pierced, you would have been born that way." I felt desperate and jealous of all the other girls I saw with beautiful jewels decorating their ears.

One of the girls from the home meetings said she knew how to pierce ears with a needle. I was so tempted, thinking about how pretty I would look with earrings. But I thought about what Dad said, so I did not do it. I told him about it, and he was proud of me that I had resisted temptation.

I wondered why we had to be different. Other kids at school had nice things, they were happy, and their parents had normal jobs. I stuck out. I was different, and everything we did at home—the praying, the singing, and the home meetings— these made me feel like even more of an oddity.

So, of course, I was bullied. Kids teased me for the clothes I wore. I did not have any friends at school. I sat alone at lunch. I was called "Macho Nacho" a lot.

There was one particular boy who called me names. He happened to walk home from school the same way I did. Sometimes he would even throw rocks at me for fun. I told Dad about it, and he said I should do what Jesus would do—show kindness to someone who was a bully and turn the other cheek. I wanted to try it out, to see if it would work.

The next day, I thought of something nice to say to this boy if he started the name calling. Sure enough, when we were walking home, the teasing started.

"Hey, Macho Nacho," he said. "Where did you find those rags you're wearing?"

He snickered, and I heard a rock tap against the sidewalk and soon others pelted my heel. I started to do what I usually did—walk a little faster so I could get away from him. But, I remembered I wanted to turn the other cheek today. I nervously glanced back at him and noticed he was carrying an oversized paper in his hand. In between his name-calling, I asked sweetly, "What is that you have?"

He eyed me as if wondering if he should be suspicious of me. But he replied, "It's just a picture I drew in art class."

"Let me see it," I said in my friendliest voice.

We stopped in the middle of the sidewalk, hesitating a second, and then he showed me the picture, still seeming wary of me. It was a drawing of an outdoor scene: grass and sky and water in colorful hues.

"It's beautiful," I said. "Did you do it all by yourself?"

He looked shocked. "Yeah, I did that." His voice sounded pleased.

"That's really good," I said.

He did not seem to know what to say. We walked the rest of the way to our houses in silence. He did not call me Macho Nacho the rest of the way. He did not call my clothes rags. But he did wave slightly to me, and smiled when he got to his house. The next day when we walked home, he did not call me names or throw rocks at me, and he never did again.

Dad was proud of me; he beamed when I told him about it, but it was a small victory. The other kids still teased me, and I pretended I was sick a lot so I would not have to endure their taunts.

I was in sixth grade, and finally Dad and Mom decided to home school me. I was relieved. I was twelve, and for all Dad's strictness and *godly ways*, I wanted to be like Lynne and Lilly. There was a fight going on inside of me: part of me wanted to please Mom and Dad, and part of me wanted to be normal—be like my older sisters.

I wanted to style my hair, poof up my bangs like the other kids did and not wear it straight and long down my back with bangs bluntly cut across my forehead. I took some of my paper route money, and with Mom's permission, I beamed all the way to the only hair salon in town. I wanted a modern cut so I could fit in at school.

The hair stylist cut my hair way too short. I cried a little, thinking to myself: I wish I had asked Dad instead of Mom about going to get a hair makeover. He surely would have said no to a new hairdo, and now it would take me forever to grow it back out; she had cut almost all of my hair off. I felt that I had learned my lesson the hard way as I studied myself in the mirror.

I also wanted to wear fashionable clothes, jeans with name-brands sewn on the back pocket; not the old Lees that Mom got from the clothing drive. No wonder I was teased all the time.

I wanted to take my cues from Lynne and Lilly. I still got to see them once in a while, though Dad would not have approved if he had known. I asked Mom for permission when Dad was out doing one of his odd jobs, and she usually said yes.

Lynne and Lilly would take me out to eat, which was fun, because we could not afford it at home. They would always let me watch movies and listen to rock and roll music. They even did my hair and makeup. I had to be careful to wash it off before I went back home. However, my visits with my older sisters were few and far between.

Of course, I did not always ask permission to see them. Sometimes I snuck out on my own. There was an old nature trail that ran all the way from Center Point to Cedar Rapids, not far from the apartment where Lynne and Pat lived.

One summer day, I took the trail on my bike, enjoying the feel of the sun on my face and the wind blowing through my hair. I relished the freedom I felt. It took me hours to get there, but I did not mind. I arrived at Lynne and Pat's apartment at night.

I knew Mom and Dad were probably looking for me, but I did not want to go home. I wanted to spend the night with Lynne. After a phone call to Dad, begging him to let me stay, I did get to spend the night, to my delight. I stayed up all night watching all the movies I could — the kind of movies I could not watch at home: Rain Man, Die Hard, and The Terminator. These movies had always been off limits since they were full of swearing, sex and killing.

Lynne made popcorn and sat on the couch next to me, and we watched movies the entire night, not going to sleep until four in the morning. Mom and Dad were at Lynne's bright and early to pick me up and take me back home. Of course, I was then in trouble.

Dad sent me to my room and made me read the Bible to find out what I had done wrong and why God did not want me to do those worldly things. I did not understand why watching movies and hanging out with my sister was so wrong. But, I quoted some verses from the Bible, and Dad seemed to be satisfied.

Surprisingly, after that, Dad let me go to Lynne and Lilly's, but only once in a while. I guess he figured if I was going to sneak out and go anyway, I might as well be safe and have them take me instead.

Whenever I went, I did the usual things—things I could not do at home. I always watched movies voraciously, any movies I could get my hands on. When I stayed with Lilly, she showed me her makeup drawer, and I admired the eye shadows and lipsticks and blushes. It was new and exciting to me. She decorated my face for me, and I never knew why Dad always thought it was wrong to wear makeup. I loved the way Lilly did my hair, fluffing it up in the current style. I admired myself in her mirror, my face painted and my hair done. I thought I actually looked hot. I wanted to look like that all of the time.

Lynne and Lilly always asked how things were at home. They hoped that Dad would quit being so religious and get a real job. They remembered how life used to be before, though I did not know any different. They thought maybe Dad was just going through a phase, and one day, he would go back to life as it was before religion took over. None of us knew then that life would never be as it was, and things would only get worse.

At Lynne's apartment, there was a pool. She had stylish bikinis, and she shared her favorites with me as we laid out in the sun on the swimming pool deck. We would read novels as we got a suntan. Lynne always asked if I had a boyfriend, and the answer was invariably the same. Dad would never let me have a boyfriend.

There had been a boy once that I had had a crush on for a year, and I knew he liked me too. His name was Ron. Dad would never allow me to spend time with the boy, and I knew that, so I told Dad that I had to babysit. Instead, I met the boy at the store and we went for a walk, holding hands together.

It felt good to hold his hand, even if it was a little sweaty. It was the first real contact, real touching, that I had ever had with a boy. When we got back to the store, he even gave me a kiss. It was just a quick peck on the lips, but it was a real kiss from a real boy, and in that moment, he was my boyfriend. It did not last for long though.

Dad pulled up in his car, saw us holding hands, saw the kiss, and ordered me to get into the car. I did not know that he had gone to check on me and had not found me babysitting and was looking for me the entire time. Those were the end of my babysitting days. It was also the end of boys for me. My next experience would not come until I was nineteen.

Even though I was not allowed to see boys, I still wanted to be attractive. I admired Lynne and Lilly's beautiful, tanned skin, and liked the experience I had laying with Lynne next to the pool.

I wanted my skin to be tan, too, and I was determined to do it at home. I found an old swimsuit that one of the twins had left, put some lotion on, and laid a towel down on the side of the house where the sun was shining. It felt wonderful to feel the sun on my skin and know that I was going to have a beautiful tan like my older sisters. But it was not long before a shadow blocked out the sun — Dad had found me.

"What are you doing?" he demanded.

"I'm getting a sun tan," I said. I wanted to add, "like Lynne and Lilly," but I thought better of it.

"Get up," he firmly ordered me, and I had to obey. "Put some clothes on; that swimsuit is too revealing."

I looked down at the suit. It was a one piece that covered every inch of my torso from my hips to my neck, so I did not understand how it could be too revealing.

"What you're doing is not of God," Dad continued. "You're sinning; you're being vain." He told me to go to my room and pray, read the

Bible, and see what I was doing that offended God. But, as usual, I never understood what I was doing wrong.

Dad took the swimsuit, and I never saw it again. But that was not the end. Soon, more things would be taken from me.

I also wanted my hair to look like Lynne and Lilly's, platinum blonde. Dad would not allow me to color it, of course, because that would be a sin in God's eyes.

I snuck into the bathroom and grabbed some bleach and peroxide thinking I could dye my hair quietly when no one was watching. Dad saw me acting strange, so he approached me on the front porch and asked what I was doing with bleach tucked behind my back, and why did my hair smell funny? I had to march up to my room that instant and repent for my hair dye attempt.

At that time, I idolized the older twins and how popular and pretty they looked with their designer clothes. Dad was trying to break me from this thinking by sending me to my room to repent before God.

Five

Dad's favorite thing to say was, "God will provide." This not only applied to material things, but with our health, as well. We were not allowed to go to the doctor. In fact, I did not even know people were supposed to get a yearly physical until I was an adult. I never had one myself growing up. If any of us ever got sick, Dad would pray over us, and Mom would rely on home remedies like chicken noodle soup or bathing us in cold water for a fever.

Luckily, I was never too sick, but Mom was not so lucky. I did not realize how serious things were until the summer I was twelve.

Mom was in the kitchen washing dishes, and I came in from outside to see if she needed help with anything. Since Lynne moved out, I had become her best little helper, and I was proud of it. I sat at the kitchen table and watched her for a while as she moved in the rhythm of washing a dish, rinsing a dish, placing a dish in the rack to dry. She sang hymns as she worked, songs I had heard many times during our prayer meetings.

"What do you need help with Mom?" I finally asked.

She did not answer me. Mom was not singing anymore. She seemed to hesitate for a moment, and then I watched her slide to the ground in slow motion, and I heard her hissing like a cat. I nervously ran over to her, kneeling down beside her still body.

"Mom, are you okay?" I asked, touching her. I shook her gently, calling her name again, asking if she was okay, but she did not respond to me, and now she was foaming at the mouth and this scared me. I ran and found Dad. He was in the prayer room. Even though I was not supposed to disturb him there, I did not care, I knew this was an emergency.

"Dad," I screamed, rushing into the room. He was sitting on a chair; his prayer shawl wrapped around him snuggly. He opened his eyes and gave me a stern look, ready to reprimand me, but before he could open his mouth, I blurted out, "Mom fell. She's lying on the kitchen floor."

He stood up quickly, rushing to the kitchen, but when he got there, he turned around, blocking the doorway. "Don't come in," he said.

"But—"

He pointed to the stairs. "Go to your room and pray," he instructed.

I reluctantly obeyed him. I was so worried about Mom. I was even more anxious when the ambulance arrived in the driveway. I watched out my window as two men walked across the lawn to the porch steps, then disappeared from view. I heard them talking downstairs, but I could not make out their words.

I did not know if it was serious or not. I wanted to know what was happening with Mom and if she was going to be all right. A while later, I saw the two men leave again, and I knew Mom must be okay because she was not with them.

I later found out that what Mom had experienced was a seizure. She had experienced them before, but this was the first time I had witnessed one. Mom's older sister, Judi, told me later that the seizures had started when Mom was pregnant with my sister, Conny; she once had rheumatic fever while pregnant, and this turned into Sydenham's chorea when Conny was born. Sydenham's Chorea causes a person to lose muscle control in their limbs causing sporadic movements and muscle twitching. Sydenham's chorea can lead to epilepsy later in life which can be controlled with medicine.

Jess and Conny both had seen her seizing. It was always the same — Mom slumping to the floor and hissing with foam coming out of her mouth. It scared them, just like it scared me.

Mom had medication to prevent her from having the seizures, but she did not take it. Dad would not allow her to. The medicine was called Dilantin. He said that God would cure her, and she did not need the medicine.

One afternoon when Mom had a seizure, I was in the kitchen with her. She was at the table, a glass of water and her pill bottle in front of her. She fiddled with the pill bottle nervously, opening and closing the cap, as if trying to decide if she should take one or not. Soon I heard heavy footsteps in the hallway, and Dad came in holding his Bible. He saw Mom at the table and noticed the pill bottle in front of her. His faced morphed into anger.

"Go play outside," he shouted at me. I reluctantly did as he said and walked out into the hallway. He shut the kitchen door behind me, but I was curious about what he was going to do. So I tiptoed back and peeked through the key hole. I watched him push the pill bottle and the water aside and put the Bible in their place. Mom closed her eyes and bowed her head down, and he put his hand on her head and started to pray over her.

"God, cure this woman from the ailment she suffers. You cured the blind man and gave him sight. You cured the lepers and made the lame walk again." Dad went on and on like that, imploring God to make her seizures go away.

I watched for a few minutes, but I must have made a noise, because Dad suddenly glared towards the door, and I quickly ran off before he found me. I went outside to the backyard with the image of Dad praying over Mom, trying to cure her of her seizures while her real cure, the pills, were pushed to the side, forbidden.

Dad believed he had cured her. That is

until the next time she had a seizure. Then the pattern would repeat itself: Mom would consider taking her medication, Dad would pray over her, she would be "cured," then she would have a seizure, and it would start all over again. It seemed to be a vicious cycle.

During all of this, I never realized how much pain Mom was in, how much she suffered. She hid it well behind her smiles and laughs, and she went on with her daily life. She loved spending time in the kitchen or outside in her garden, and increasingly, that's where I spent my time with her. We kept the chickens in the backyard, and I would help her care for them, feeding them and gathering their eggs.

In the summer, there were the gardens to tend to, and in the fall, there was canning to do. And soon I found myself constantly helping her in the kitchen. She would let me help her make the dinner or stir the cookie dough for desert.

I was thirteen and felt like I was getting closer to her. It was a different kind of closeness, not the kind you feel when you're a child, but a deeper understanding and connection that you feel as you become an adult. But beneath it all, there was always the pain, the suffering that she never let on was there.

I think she tried to tell me one time. It was May, and she and I were inside watering the flowers. She was showing me how to give them just enough water so the dirt was moist but not saturated.

"I'll be glad when I won't have to work so hard," she said, gently pouring a cup of water onto some African violets, "and there won't be any pain or suffering. I'll be in a happy place." She looked at me and smiled, but her eyes were looking past me, not at me, like she was envisioning a place where she would not suffer.

I figured she was talking about heaven and the Bible and the suffering everyone goes through on Earth. It was something Dad would preach about at the home meetings. So I shrugged off what she said and did not give it much more thought.

Summer came quickly after that, and soon there were flowers outside to care for as well as the ones in the house. One day in June, Mom and I spent the day pulling weeds in the garden, and then I helped her make dinner.

"Crack the eggs like this," she said, showing me how to tap them on the bowl and open them without breaking the yolk. We were making quiche. She cut the ham and bacon into tiny pieces and let me sprinkle them in and mix it all together. She snuck in a few vegetables too, just like she always did in the dinners. Lettuce on peanut butter sandwiches, or celery in the spaghetti sauce: she always made sure we got our vegetables. She was such a thoughtful Mom.

"Now pour it in gently," she instructed, and I carefully tipped the bowl, watching the mixture slide into the pie crust. She put it in the oven, and I sat in front of it, watching it bubble and rise in the heat. That evening at dinner, Dad commented about how good everything tasted and I felt proud.

It was warm one night when we went to bed, and we opened the windows. I listened as Dad read a Bible story to Rebekah and me, like he did every night. He usually read to the three of us, but Jon was sleeping at a friend's house, so it was just Rebekah and I that night, listening to the soothing sounds of Dad's voice. I was grateful for the breeze that rustled the curtains and tickled my cheeks and neck.

Dad finished the story and said a few words about what it meant and how it applied to our life. Then he tucked us in and turned out the lights. I heard him shuffle downstairs to watch the news with Mom, and I started to drift off to sleep, listening to the sounds of the crickets chirping outside the open window.

I woke up in a cold sweat, I do not know how much later, to the sound of banging. I looked around, confused, wondering what the noise was and where it was coming from. I sat up in bed and glanced over at Rebekah. She was sleeping soundly. The banging noise continued, but now I heard a loud crashing too, like something had fallen to the floor and broken. I swung my legs off the bed and walked barefoot across the floor, listening for a moment at the door before opening and poking my head into the hallway. Dad was yelling now, and all the banging and crashing noises were coming from their bedroom.

"Do something!" Dad shouted. "You can move mountains, heal her! Do something right now!"

I ran to their room and stood in the open doorway. "Is everything okay?" I gasped, surveying the scene before me. Dad was hovering over Mom on the bed, his Bible in his hand, one fist in the air, shouting at God.

Mom was having a seizure, her arms and legs flailing around. The evidence of her seizure was lying all over the floor — a lamp, her knick knacks from the nightstand table, the clock — all lay broken and scattered around the bed. Her body was making the bed shake, causing the headboard to knock against the wall — the banging sound that had woke me up.

"Everything's fine," Dad said, "go back to your room."

I walked down the hallway towards my bedroom. I was wondering if Dad was going to call the ambulance this time, and I was wondering if Mom was going to be okay. I was so confused, thinking that something awful was happening, and then, all of a sudden, everything went quiet.

"Blessing," Dad shouted, piercing the still eerie silence that seemed to surround us.

I sprinted back to the room. Mom was lying hauntingly motionless across the bed, face down now. Her head was slumped off of the bed, and blood was running out of her mouth, pooling on the spotless floor beneath her. I stared, transfixed at the blood, thinking how scarlet red it looked, how it was staining the carpet, and how Mom would have a hard time cleaning it up the next morning. I could not move a muscle, like a deer starring at headlights. I would offer to help her with it tomorrow, of course. She would be glad for my help.

"Do you know CPR?" Dad snapped me back into reality.

"Only a little," I stuttered, thinking it was a silly question to ask. Mom did not need CPR. She was just having a bad seizure, but she would be okay, she always was okay after she had her seizures.

"Call an ambulance," Dad ordered, and there was something different about his harsh voice that scared me. I should have run to the phone and dialed 911, but I was frightened and in shock, so I ran to the neighbor's house instead. I just wanted someone to tell me everything was going to be okay. I wanted them to tell me I did not need to worry.

I could not get rid of the sight of Mom's immobile body slumped over the bed. Her blood was all over the floor beneath her. Her skin was not flesh colored but had a strange whitish-blue tint. This image was something imprinted into my mind for life. I could not shake the sight of my Mom, motionless. I felt helpless.

I rang the doorbell, and as I waited, I thought about how Dad would not want me to be at the neighbor's house. He had started to crack down on my friendships, and Shannon was one of the friends he did not let me play with anymore. I would probably have to apologize and pray about what I had done wrong.

I started to think maybe I should go back home, but the door opened and Shannon's Mom stood there in her nightgown and robe. Seeing her reassured me. Mothers were supposed to answer doors late at night and help you when you needed it. They did not have seizures and cough up blood and die.

"Blessing," she greeted me, smiling, but she must have seen my face because she immediately looked concerned. "What is it, honey?"

"Dad says to call the ambulance," I blurted. It was all I could get out, my whole body now shaking. I had done my duty — someone was getting an ambulance. Now, I wanted to go back home, see Mom, and make sure she was okay.

But she was not okay when I got back to her bedroom. She was on the floor, Dad straddling her, his hands on her chest doing compressions. I stood in the doorway, numb and in shock. Mom looked white, and I did not like seeing her look that way. She did not look like Mom anymore. I closed my eyes, but I could not get the image out of my head. Mom was white, lying on the floor, dark blood smeared on her cheeks, too much blood.

A few moments later, heavy footsteps pounded up the stairs. The men from the ambulance had arrived, ready to save Mom. I was happy to go to my own bedroom to be out of the way. I was relieved that Mom was going to be okay now.

Rebekah was still asleep in our room. It was hard to believe all of the chaos had not awakened her. I lay in my bed, listening to the crickets again, trying to pretend that nothing had happened.

All I remember was that Dad had just finished reading us a book. He and Mom were downstairs watching the news. Soon they went upstairs to bed, and we were all going to drift off to sleep. In the morning, we would all wake up, and Mom would have breakfast for us. I fell asleep in the sweet arms of denial—this was all a bad dream, and everything would be fine when I woke up in the morning. My heavy eyelids drooped shut.

The next morning, the sun was shining bright, it seemed like a cheerful day, and I knew Mom had to be okay. I could almost smell the blueberry muffins that she was making. I skipped downstairs to see mom, wanting to tell her about the bad dream I had had the night before, the dream where she had had another seizure, the dream that she was frozen white, and there was blood all over the floor, and Dad was trying to revive her. She would give me a hug and tell me it was all a nightmare.

When I entered the family room, Dad was sitting in the prayer chair with the prayer cloak over him. He was not moving. He was not talking. He was not praying. He just sat there, staring at the wall.

"She's gone," he mumbled when he saw me. That was it, two simple words: she's gone. And then I knew the previous night had really happened. It was not the nightmare I hoped it was. It was like a slap to the face. My heart just sank to the floor. I felt numb inside thinking, where is God now? Why had He not saved Mom? She had done nothing wrong.

I should have cried, but I did not. I should have believed him, but I could not. I did not want to. Instead, I walked into the kitchen to find her. I paused in the doorway, not wanting to look in. If she was not in there, I would know Dad was telling the truth. I clung to the moment, hanging onto the hope that Dad had been mistaken. As long as I stood in the doorway and did not look in, then I was fine. I could stand there all day and Mom could still be alive.

Slowly, I forced myself to take a step forward and look, look to see if Mom was making breakfast like she did every morning or if she really was not there. I discovered that Dad was right. She was gone. The realization that she was gone hit me hard and sudden. I was too traumatized and too upset to feel anything except emptiness, like there was a large hole in the middle of my chest. My heart felt all twisted in knots and my breathing became erratic. I missed her, and I knew then that I would miss her every day, for the rest of my life.

The events of the rest of that day were a blur. I was aware that Dad called my older brothers and sisters to tell them the news because they all trickled in later that day. I heard him talk to Lynne on the phone and ask her to come over and help pick out an outfit for Mom to wear in the casket. When she arrived that afternoon with her eyes red, Dad told her she could go through Mom's things and see if there was anything she wanted. She went upstairs but was back down again after a few minutes.

"What's this?" she asked in an accusing voice, waving a bottle of pills in front of Dad's face. He still sat in his prayer chair, head down, but he lifted it slowly and stared up at her.

"Where did you find those?" he asked quietly.

I knew what they were. I had seen them before; they were Mom's pills, the ones she never took because Dad had forbidden it. He said she did not need them. Supposedly, God had healed her, except that God really had not.

"I found them in the closet upstairs,"

Lynne replied. "They were hidden behind some sweaters. They're expired. Why wasn't she taking them?"

"She didn't need them," Dad said. "We prayed about it. God said she didn't need to take them anymore. God was her healer."

"She did need them," she shouted, holding the bottle of pills threateningly. I thought she was going to throw them at him, but instead she hurled them at the floor. "All your praying to God didn't heal her. She was sick, and now she's dead."

I remembered the time, just last summer, when I had seen Dad push her pills aside and pray over her with the Bible. It was always that way. Dad always thought that God would heal us when we were sick. I always believed him for some reason. However, I did not believe him now. I felt angry at Dad, but I was even angrier at God.

"Why did you take her?" I asked God in the privacy of my room. "It's not fair."

I glared at the cross hanging on the wall and the picture of Jesus in the hall just outside my room. I thought if God was a true God, then why did He take my mother? She was the best mom, and we kids needed her. How would we get by without our Mother?

"Why didn't you take a murderer or a drug dealer? Why take someone good?" I prayed.

I could not get an answer, just silence,

always silence. Why could I not hear God when I needed Him the most?

More relatives came: aunts and uncles, cousins, grandparents. I sat on the front porch and watched them walking up to the house. Some were cousins from Minnesota that I barely knew. What I did know was that *they* still had their mothers.

Mom's mother was upset with Dad, believing he pushed religion too far, and she barely spoke a word to him the whole time. I think inwardly, she blamed Dad for mom's death. Since there was no way to prove it, just a full pill bottle of Mom's medication, she kept quiet and just gave Dad cold looks while she was there for the funeral.

Dad was in such a dazed, depressed state that he did not seem to notice much, up until the funeral. He sat in his prayer chair with a shabby old cloak hanging around his shoulders and looked at his open Bible in his lap. He stared at it as if he were staring straight through it. I was worried about him. He had not moved from his prayer chair since Mom's death, not even to eat or check on us.

I probably should have been mad at him too, like Grandma was, but for some reason, at that very instant, I felt sorry for him in his state of mourning. I felt like Dad really thought that since God could move mountains like the Bible says, then surely God could heal Mom of her seizures too.

At that time, I did not blame him for Mom's death. I was not angry with him either. That would all come later, when Mom's absence sunk in. But, in that instant, I was having a hard time realizing Mom was never coming back, at least not in this lifetime.

The next day, there was the wake. It was held in a tiny town hall in Whittier, Iowa. Almost the entire town had been baptized and saved previously when Dad and many elders conducted a charismatic revival that had swept through the town. I was barely old enough to remember, but it all came back to me. Many people were saved with Dad's preaching, and now, they were all gathered in quiet reverence at Mom's funeral service.

I did not want to go — did not want to see Mom lying in a casket. It would make it all too official for me. I could still pretend that this was all a dream, pretend that this never happened. If I saw her in the casket, saw her being buried, I knew there would be no going back.

Everyone was sad and crying at the wake. I stood at the back of the room, glancing sideways at the coffin in the front, not wanting to approach it. It was a simple one, Dad not able to afford anything fancy. An elder friend of Dad's was a woodworker and volunteered to make Mom's coffin. It was a labor of kindness for a mother that had shared the gospel with so many, in a generous, considerate manner, always giving unto others even if it had meant the last bit of food we had in the kitchen. This was the least the elder could do with his woodworking skills. It turned out to be a very unique and beautiful casket with marbled wooden inlays throughout.

Out of the corner of my eye, I could see the profile of Mom's face above the side of the casket. I turned my body so as not to see her, I just could not look at her. I kept thinking to myself, this is not happening, she is still alive and waiting at home.

Suddenly, I was caught up in a line of relatives who ushered me to the front, bidding me to say goodbye to her. Each step I took brought me closer, my heart pounding. I did not want to go up there. I could see flashbacks of her lying over the bed, blood racing out of her mouth, deep, dark and red. I had never seen so much blood in my life, and the last person I had ever wanted to see in such a state was my mom.

I shook my head to clear my thoughts. I tried to turn away and go back, but my relatives pressed me. Then, there I was, looking at her, except it did not seem like her, it did not look like her at all. They had put too much makeup on her. Mom never wore makeup except on rare special occasions like her and Dad's wedding anniversary. She was white, oh so white, I did not like it.

Lynne had done a good job of picking out her outfit, but the scarf she wore was tied all wrong. Mom always tied it like a bowtie, and they had tied it like a man's tie. I wanted to reach over and fix it for her—she would not have liked it that way, but I did not. I kept my hands still. I could not move. I just froze in place. I felt all mushy inside, a lump forming in the pit of my stomach.

"That's not Mom," I shouted loudly, wanting people to hear and agree with me, but no one said anything or even looked up at me. I fumed inside. I did not want to be there. All I could think about was that there was no way that that was Mom.

There were a lot of people at the wake: friends, relatives, and old church members. I overheard Dad talking to one of his friends, an Elder from his old church. "I'm not sure she made it," Dad said with a twinge of sadness in his voice.

"What do you mean?" the man asked, surprised.

"Heaven," Dad replied. "I'm not sure she made it to heaven."

I did not understand, and I felt angry. How could Dad think that? Mom was the best person I had ever known, the best Mom and the best Christian. How could he think she had not made it to heaven? She was so unselfish, so kind and caring to others, especially us kids. She loved us with all of her heart.

I could not stop thinking about how much I missed her, and just then, the tears came running like a river down my face. My oldest sister, Conny, with her flashy black designer dress, came over and embraced me tight. Tears flooded both our faces now.

Our Mom breathed and lived every day for us. I already missed her terribly more than I could ever imagine. It had only been a few days since she had left us. She died Monday evening, June 6, 1988, at Mercy Hospital in Cedar Rapids, Iowa. She was 45 years old.

After my experience at the wake, I did not want to go to the funeral. I did not want to picture her under the ground, in the dirt. I wanted to picture her alive, like she had been. So I stayed home and wished I could see her again. I got my wish a few weeks later. I was very upset and distraught, and I wanted everyone to leave so things could go back to normal, like before, when Mom was alive.

It was the middle of the day. I had been outside, trying to play, but playing was not easy for me anymore. I felt I was betraying Mom by having fun, so I came in the house.

It was quiet when I entered; I knew Dad was out on a job, and Jon and Rebekah were both outside. I was alone in the house. At least, that is what I thought. I was just about to walk upstairs when I heard a noise in the laundry room. I paused at the bottom step and glanced over, and there was Mom, doing the laundry like she always did, like nothing had ever happened. I felt an immediate relief. Mom was alive; it had all been a nightmare, just like I thought.

"Mom!" I said excitedly, calling her.

She did not respond to me. I continued to call for her, feeling frustrated that she was not acknowledging me. She did not even look at me. She just put the laundry in the washing machine, set the lid down and turned away, heading down to the cellar.

She looked actual flesh and blood color, not ghostly at all. She had on her favorite striped blouse she loved to wear and the same old worn blue jeans that she never put down. I followed her to the cellar, but when I got down there, I could not find her anywhere. I was immediately deflated. My heart sank, and I knew then that she was gone, and she was never coming back.

I never saw her again after that. I looked and looked everywhere, but to no avail, she was definitely gone. I did not understand why I was the only one to see her. When I asked Jon or Rebekah if they had seen her too, they both looked at me strange and shook their heads no. How peculiar, I thought to myself.

Even though I was sad, seeing her made me feel better, because I knew she was in a better place. It comforted me to know she was not in the ground, under layers of dirt. Seeing her helped me to start to move on.

For Mom, the pain and suffering had ended, but for me, it was just beginning. Soon after Mom's death, Conny was in Mom's bedroom and happened to find Dad's journal, the one where he wrote about his visions and dreams.

She told me about a dream he had written down before Mom died, a dream about a dark-haired woman standing on the other side of a river, calling for him to come over to her. He was not sure if it was right or not, but he crossed the water to this dark-haired woman. And soon this dark-haired woman would really enter our lives.

Six

Dad met Cheri before Mom died, at a church in Cedar Rapids that we sometimes attended in addition to our home meetings. Dad was known among the church-goers as a handyman. He could do just about anything: plumbing, simple electrical work, carpet installation, or painting. One day after church service, a dark-haired woman approached Dad, introduced herself as Cheri, and asked him for help fixing her washing machine. Dad was glad to help; he needed the work. The small amount she would pay him would put food on our table for a couple of days.

A few days later, Dad and Mom and the three of us kids packed into the old station-wagon and drove to Cheri's house in Cedar Rapids. Dad immediately got to work while Cheri and Mom visited in the kitchen. Cheri had plants all around her house, just like Mom, and the two women seemed to have a lot in common as they talked about the Bible. Cheri even had three kids, two boys and a girl, similar in ages to Jon, Rebekah and me. Tom was twelve, a year younger than me; Emily, at ten, was the same age as Jon; and Allen was six like Rebekah.

Emily and I immediately clicked, though she was three years younger than me. We entertained ourselves in the basement, playing with her dolls. Even though we did not stay long that day, I felt like I had made a new best friend.

It was only about a month later that Cheri contacted Dad again, this time needing help with a pipe that was leaking under the kitchen sink. We all piled into the car, happily going to Cheri's house. I was excited to play with Emily again, I had not seen her since the last time we went to their house.

We stayed longer this time, Dad and Mom and Cheri discussing scripture after Dad fixed the leaky pipe. Cheri even invited us to stay for dinner, and the nine of us squeezed around the table, though Cheri's cooking was nothing compared to Mom's. That was the last we saw of Cheri for a few months.

After Mom died, Dad stopped going to church and home meetings for a while. He would sit in his prayer chair with a cloak over him all day long, not moving and not speaking. He was in a deep depression. I thought he looked horrible, I had never seen him look that bad.

That first week after Mom was gone, people came over to make sure us kids were taken care of and had some food to eat, since Dad was practically incapacitated. Neighbors would come by with a hot dish or friends from the home meetings would stop over and do some light cleaning.

They noticed that all Dad did was sit in his prayer chair, probably not moving since the last time they had been there. After a week or two of this, people started to encourage him to pull himself together, take care of us kids and go to church again. They said that going to church would make him feel better.

It was at the end of June, Mom had only been gone for a few weeks, when Dad brought Cheri and her children home after a church service.

"You remember Cheri and the kids," Dad said to me. His eyes were bright, and he actually had a slight smile on his face. He did not quite look happy yet, but at least he did not seem as depressed anymore.

I was elated to see Emily again.

"Cheri and I are going to do some Bible study," Dad announced. "You kids go and play."

We left Cheri and Dad sitting in the living room together, a Bible between them, while we kids dispersed in various directions. Emily and I went outside. She had a dollar that Cheri had given her, so we walked to the store to buy candy.

"Don't you have any toys to play with?" Emily asked as we walked back to the house. She took another bite of her candy bar and looked up at me, chocolate smeared around her mouth.

She had graciously shared her money with me, buying me a candy bar too, which I quickly gobbled down. It had been a long time since I had the luxury of eating a candy bar.

"We have some matchbox cars," I replied, feeling embarrassed. We did not have enough money to buy things like toys. The money we did have went to pay for food to eat and a house to live in. Toys were just another luxury, like candy bars.

"I'll bring my dolls next time," Emily offered, and I was grateful to her. I realized I did not need to feel bad or embarrassed around her.

"I do have catalogs," I said, thinking about the old catalogs I had rescued from the garbage and the couple of magazines I had gotten from Lynne and Lilly, safely hidden under my bed.

"What do you do with those?" Emily asked.

"I look through them," I explained.

It was one of my favorite activities, looking through the catalogs and picking out the stylish clothing or fashionable accessories I liked. It had become one of my favorite games, allowing myself to choose only one thing per page. It became Emily's favorite activity too. That day we went through a couple of catalogs while Dad and Cheri did their Bible study together downstairs.

A few days later, Cheri was back for more Bible study with Dad while we kids played together again. "Look what I have," Emily said to me, holding out a large toy catalog from the previous Christmas.

I had never seen such a huge catalog before, and I eagerly took it from her. "Where did you get it?" I asked.

"Mom had it with some of her magazines," she replied.

We took it up to the bedroom that I shared with Rebekah, spending hours hungrily pouring over the toys, picking out which items we would like to have. There were toys in the catalog I had never seen before, toys that I did not even know how to play with or how they worked. They were all beautiful. My eyes lit up with each colorful page we turned.

Dad increasingly spent more time with Cheri which meant I got to spend more time with Emily. I did not mind Dad being with Cheri at first, it made him brighter and happier. I did not like seeing him so hopelessly depressed after Mom died. Now that Cheri was around, I felt like he was Dad again, the smile and twinkle was back in his eyes.

Sometimes we would go to Cheri's house, but more and more, Cheri was coming to our house. There was a room downstairs off the living room, it had always been Dad's prayer room, and that is where Cheri and Dad spent most of their time doing their Bible study. They spent hours and hours together, reading Bible verses. During these times, we were ordered to go play.

It was not long before Cheri and her kids moved in with us with Cheri and Dad taking over the prayer room downstairs and converting it into a bedroom. I was young and innocent and was having too much fun playing with Emily on those hot July days to realize that things had gotten romantic between Dad and Cheri. It was not until August that I began to notice.

Dad and Cheri were in the prayer room, as usual. They seemed to spend half the day in there sometimes, going over the Bible. I had a question I needed to ask Dad, so I knocked on the closed door. It was quiet within, and no one called out for me to come in. I figured Dad and Cheri were studying so intently that they had not heard me, so I opened the door.

I was shocked by what greeted me. Dad and Cheri were lying on the bed, holding and kissing each other while half undressed. I stood there for a few seconds before they noticed me. When they saw me, they quickly sat up in bed.

"You're supposed to be playing," Dad said to me, frowning.

"I'm sorry," I replied. "I just had a—"

"Go out and shut the door," he ordered, not letting me finish. "Don't bother us when we're in here."

I left and shut the door, not getting my

question answered. But I could not even remember what my question was anymore. All I could think about was Dad and Cheri, kissing and holding each other, and Mom had not even been gone two months. I was stunned by what I saw.

I was never told about the birds and the bees. When I got my period for the first time, a few months prior, Mom had not forewarned me, and I thought I would bleed to death when I saw the blood trickle down my leg. Mom got me a sanitary napkin and told me briefly that it was no big deal, just something that happened to all young women. I could not help but wonder what else I would have to look forward to as I grew up. I quickly discarded those thoughts, happy now that I was not dying, and I placed the pad where Mom showed me, cleaning myself up with the warm cloth she handed me.

Emily told me that Cheri was looking for a good husband, that is why they were going to a lot of churches after Cheri's divorce. I guess she found Dad to be her next prospect.

After Cheri moved in, we were not allowed to talk about Mom anymore. We could not even speak her name. Mom's stuff was boxed up too, but not all of it. Shortly after Cheri moved in, Mom's stuff started disappearing.

One of the first things I noticed that was gone was her sheepskin throw. Mom used to keep it at the end of her bed, and I loved laying on it. It was soft and smelled like her. She said someday, when I was older, I could have it. I looked forward to it being mine one day. After she died, it was even more important that I have it—it was something that would connect us together. But almost immediately upon Cheri's arrival into our lives, I noticed the sheepskin throw was missing.

"Where's Mom's sheepskin throw?" I asked Cheri one day. I knew they had boxed up Mom's stuff, but I did not know what they had done with all the boxes. I figured it was time I had the sheepskin; I knew Mom would want me to have it.

"It's put away," Cheri said curtly. "You don't need it, and you won't be talking about her anymore either."

I was so stunned, I could not even respond. I could not talk about my Mom anymore?

"You can remember the good times in your heart," she continued. "The good memories are something you can carry with you forever."

And that was that: no more talking about Mom. We knew if we did, we would get into trouble. Dad would yell, say we were sinning, and we would have to go to our room to ask for forgiveness and figure out what we had done wrong by reading the Bible. I never thought talking about your dead parent would be wrong in God's eyes, and I was beginning to wonder who this God was.

I was also becoming increasingly aware that God seemed to take Cheri's side. If there was something Cheri wanted to do or wanted to have, or if there was something her kids wanted, God seemed to want it for them too.

One day in August, Cheri and Emily and I were clothes shopping at a garage sale. There was a pair of jeans I spotted on one of the tables, and I went over to look at them. They had little leather ties at the bottom and on the back pockets, which made a stylish decoration. I held them up, admiring them, wanting to ask Cheri to buy them for me. Emily saw them too.

"These are cool," she said, fingering the ties on the bottom. "I think they'd fit me."

"They'd be a little too long on you," I said. Although Emily was three years younger than me she was tall for her age, and we ended up being almost the same size.

"I'm going to tell Mom about them," she said. She found Cheri and brought her back to where the jeans lay, asking if she could buy them. Right away, I protested, but Cheri prayed about it and said, "God wants Emily to have them."

My heart deflated, and I wondered again about this God who never seemed to let me have anything. It just did not seem fair. I could not have my mother, or my mother's things, and not even a pair of jeans at a garage sale. When we got home, Emily put the jeans in her drawer and would not let me borrow them, not once, and to think I saw them first. This was just not right to me. I was beginning to rethink my friendship with Emily.

Other things began to change after Cheri moved in. She and Dad decided we should go to public school instead of being homeschooled. I had had problems at a public school the year before with the name calling and with kids picking on me for the old, hand-me-down clothes that I wore. I was complaining and pretending to be sick so that I did not have to go to school.

Dad also thought public school was a lot of peer pressure with teens smoking, drinking, or partying instead of learning. I was homeschooled for my 6th and 7th grades. Dad was my teacher most of the time. With his engineering background, he was very smart with math and history.

I was in the 8th grade now, and had to attend a school in Cedar Rapids. Dad and Cheri drove us every morning and picked us up every afternoon. They were always together, and even though Cheri was not our Mom and had only known us a few months, she helped Dad make all the decisions about his kids.

One decision Cheri made was about my clothing. She did not like the hand-me-down clothes I wore; she thought they were still too stylish, too flashy. So instead, she made me wear plain, baggy clothes. These clothes would not show off any of the curves that I was starting to develop.

I was not allowed to do anything to my hair either. I could not curl it or put hair spray one it or even get it cut. It was long and straight with bangs that were ear length, so I had to pull it aside with a plain bobby pin. That was all I was allowed.

All of us girls were forbidden to cut our hair. Cheri said that our hair was a temple of God, and cutting it would be a sign of disrespect. Of course, I noticed that Cheri dressed nicely and did her hair. Curling it sometimes took her an hour, and I hated waiting when we were going somewhere all together. She even wore makeup. Those things were forbidden for me. but not for her.

Cheri made me quit my paper route, too. She thought I was buying too many worldly things with the money I earned and becoming too independent as a preteen. She said that I should be solely dependent on the Lord. She started to echo what Dad always liked to say, "God will provide."

We started going to a new church. Cheri made us girls wear dresses to service. There was another girl at the church about my own age. Her name was Charlotte, and I became friends with her. Charlotte went to the same school as I did.

I was ecstatic to finally have a friend in my class. It was someone to sit by at lunch, someone to walk with, someone to pass notes with and someone to help me endure the teasing.

I convinced Dad and Cheri to drop me off at her house in the mornings, and I would walk to school with her. Once Dad and Cheri had driven away, and we were safely out of sight, I would change into some of Charlotte's clothes. We were both the same size, and Charlotte was nice enough to let me wear her stylish name-brand clothing. She did my hair too, curling it and putting hair spray in it, even putting some makeup on me. We looked so much alike after our hair, makeup, and clothing were changed. The kids at school thought we were twins.

There were times when Charlotte's Mom thought I was her from behind, calling her name, thinking I was her. We both just turned and laughed, thinking it was cool we looked alike. After school, we made sure to wash the makeup off and brush any of the curls out of my hair, making me look plain and simple again. But I did not mind. I did not mind school anymore, either. It was like a taste of freedom for me, freedom from Cheri and Dad and their increasingly controlling religious ways.

Seven

One fall afternoon, only Dad was in the car when he came to pick me up at Charlotte's. I thought it strange that Cheri was not with him, she always went everywhere with him. We picked up Jon, Rebekah, and Cheri's three kids, and on the ride home, he asked us about our day at school and how things were going, which was not like him. Dad was usually quiet and not talkative at all.

I was sitting next to him in the front, and I thought he looked tense, his knuckles white as he clenched the steering wheel. I wondered what was going on, wondered what he was hiding.

As soon as we got home, I saw there was a large bonfire in the backyard. It was late October, so I did not think much of it. Dad had made bonfires before, burning branches and twigs from around the yard, adding garbage and other things from the house.

It was not until later, when I was upstairs in my bedroom, that I noticed some of my stuff was missing. My ten notebook journals from school were gone. Some fashionable clothes that my older sisters had given me, including some that I thought I had hidden, were gone. My stuffed animals and some souvenirs that Conny had gotten for me on her trips had disappeared. Also, my favorite short skirt and low-cut stylish white and black striped blouse I had bought with my hard earned paper route money was nowhere to be found.

I stomped downstairs to look for Cheri. I found her outside, watching the bonfire. I wanted to ask her where my things had gone, but I did not need to. I saw them burning in the fire. I saw other things too, things that were Mom's: her clothing, her pictures, her sheepskin throw that I had so desperately wanted. My heart suddenly felt like it was on fire too, burning along with everything else.

"Why are you doing this?" I asked Cheri, blinking away the tears from my eyes.

"Your stuff was too worldly," she sternly replied.

"You can't just come into my room and take my things," I sputtered.

"Most of this I took from you a while ago. If you didn't know it was gone right away, when I took it, then it must not have been that important to you."

I was too angry to reply. Instead I asked, "What about Mom's things?" I wondered how she was going to defend burning them.

"I've told you before to remember the good times in your heart," was her reply. "You don't need her stuff around to remember her. Besides, you have a new mom now."

A new mom, are you freaking kidding?

Four months after my real Mom died, I had a new one? Just like that, Cheri tried to erase Mom's memory from my life, erase her and try to take her place. She could never take Mom's place.

I quickly yelled, "No, no, no," at the top of my lungs, hoping Dad could hear as I turned and sped up to my room in defiance. I knew very well that Cheri would tell Dad about my stubbornness, and I would be in trouble, banished to my room to pray and ask God for forgiveness.

Fine, I thought to myself. I just wanted to be left alone and sulk in my room anyway. How dare Cheri start to think she could replace my Mom that easily!

I was devastated that she and Dad burned Mom's things, and I secretly cried about it for days. It was like losing Mom all over again. I was angry at Cheri, not only for burning Mom's things, but also for being so strict with us and taking our privileges away. She was taking Dad away, too.

In my heart, I started to hate her. She tried to win us kids over, and she was able to do it with Rebekah. This was only because she was so young and in need of a mother figure at her young age of six. I resented the way she tried to take Mom's place, resented all the little things she did that only reminded me of Mom and how much I missed her.

There were the birthday cakes that Cheri

baked, weak imitations of the beautiful designs Mom always made. There were the plants that Cheri tried to grow, but the flowers were never as big and pretty as Mom's. The dinners Cheri made were nothing compared to my Mom's. In short, Cheri was just a shadow of Mom. The only thing that made living with Cheri bearable was Emily. If Cheri and I did not get along, at least I had Emily to play with.

Things were only going to get worse. One day in November, Cheri was driving the six of us kids in the car. Dad was not with us, one of the few times he and Cheri were not together. There was a reason he was not there that day, and I would soon find out.

"I wanted to talk with you kids," Cheri said as she drove. "Your Dad and I have been praying, and we've decided we should get married."

There was no hesitation in her voice, she just came right out and said it. I was stunned. They wanted to get married? Mom had only been gone for five months, and already they wanted to get married?

"We want your permission," Cheri continued, but she looked right at me when she said it. I could feel her eyes boring into mine as she stared at me in the rearview mirror.

I did not like what I saw in her piercing glare, and I quickly looked away. There was just something not quite right about that manipulative look. It was not genuine or heartfelt like how my real Mom would have looked back at me. It was more like a cold, sinister look that I did not like one bit.

"No, no, no," I inwardly thought to myself, knowing that that was not the answer I had to give to her. As a kid, I did not have a choice.

I thought it strange that she felt she needed permission from a thirteen year old. I certainly did not want to give it to her. I wanted to scream at her to get out of our lives and leave us alone, but I could not, my lips were trembling. She would never be my mom.

In truth, I was scared of Cheri, scared of the way her eyes always looked at me. So instead, I mumbled, "Of course. I'm glad you guys are happy together."

I *was* glad that Dad was happy. He was so depressed and so sad after Mom died. Cheri at least had taken him out of his slump. But deep in my heart, I did not want them to get married. It would mean Cheri becoming my stepmom, and my heart sank at the thought. All hope was gone, I felt.

Cheri tried to win me over before she and Dad got married. She took the three of us girls to the mall in Cedar Rapids once, shortly before Christmas. We ate at one of the fast-food restaurants, and then we walked to a little store where they sold cute things like jewelry, hair accessories, purses, and socks. Of course, we were not allowed to buy any jewelry, and I still did not have my ears pierced, but that did not stop me from wishing and admiring.

"I'll buy you each a pair of socks," Cheri said. It did not sound like much, but I was excited. I could not remember the last time I had a new pair of anything. Something brand new to wear – something no one else had previously worn.

We did not get to go to the mall very much, so it was totally awesome to see the new styles displayed in the store front windows, even if it was just window shopping. We were getting out of the boring house, and I could dream about and admire all the bright, new clothes. Since I was taught that Christians did not dress that way, and we did not have enough money anyway, it was just a daydream. I could still wish and wonder. Cheri could never take that from me.

I looked over the wall of socks. There had to be at least thirty different pairs from which to choose: pink ones with words like *cool* and *fun* printed on them, white ones with rainbows, purple ones with sunglasses, and blue ones with puppies. I loved them all and wanted them all. But I could only pick one.

Of all the socks on the wall, there was one pair that caught my eye: a pale yellow pair with little lambs. For some reason, they made me think of Mom and her sheepskin throw. I knew that was the pair of socks I wanted. The only problem was, there was only one pair like it left, and Emily wanted them too.

"I was going to take those," she pouted as I slid the socks off the hook.

"I like them too," I said. I wanted to add, *I got them first*, but thought better of it. Instead, I said, "They remind me of my Mom." Of course that was the wrong thing to say. I should not have mentioned Mom. Cheri was my *mom* now; I should have remembered that.

Cheri did not say anything, but she snatched the socks from my hand and gave them to Emily. Of course, she prayed about it, and of course, God told her that Emily should have the socks. I wondered why God did not want me to have anything I wanted and why Emily always got the nicer things.

None of the other socks were good enough now. Emily had the pair that I wanted. And again, she would not ever let me wear them, just like with the jeans. I picked out a white pair with swimsuits dotted on them and went home with a lump in my throat.

Cheri and Dad were planning to get married on Christmas Eve. About a week before the wedding, Cheri took us shopping again to get dresses. We went to Montgomery Ward's in Cedar Rapids, to the bottom floor where they were having one of their bargain basement closeouts. Everything was at least half off.

I do not know where Cheri got the money to buy the dresses, but I did not care. Rebekah, Emily, and I each got a lavender dress, and

Cheri found a nice white dress to wear as the bride. I felt proud when I tried mine on in the store. I felt like a million bucks, and I waltzed around, admiring myself in the mirrors. It was the nicest thing I had ever worn.

The day before the wedding, Cheri told us that she had prayed about it, and God said it was okay, this one special time, that we would be able to have our hair curled. We did not have any curlers, so she tied our hair up in rags. That night it was hard to sleep, but the next morning when she took the rags out there were beautiful, tight curls all over my head. With the dress on, I felt like a princess.

I wished then that my Mom could have seen how pretty I looked in the lavender dress. I was not sure that I should have felt so happy about the wedding, because Mom had just died months ago. The wedding, a new stepmom: it was happening so fast that in my mind, I was having a hard time catching up. I liked that dress tremendously, but all the changes with a new Mom were almost too much for me to grasp.

I had not really grieved over Mom's death yet. I could still not shake the image out of my head of Mom lying motionless over her bed, blood spurting out of her mouth. I wanted to rewind to that moment and save her so bad, but it was too late. This memory was hard to erase, as much as I tried to get the thoughts out of my head. I wanted my real Mom back so bad that it was starting to become hard to be nice to the new stepmom. She put her kids first, giving them the nicest things first and me, Jon, and Rebekah the leftovers. I pretended to smile and be happy when she looked my way, although inside, I was hurt with a sad ball of mixed emotions.

Their wedding took place at the church we had been attending for the past few months. It was a small, simple ceremony. Lynne and Lilly were the only relatives that were there. Cherri and Dad did not want a big fancy wedding. They had purposely not invited any family members that were not of the same Christian beliefs that we were following.

Most of the family members on mom's side were still upset over mom's sudden death. She was too young, and Dad's remarriage happened much too soon.

Dad actually called Lynne on the phone. I overheard him ask her to take pictures of the wedding, since they could not afford a professional photographer. Lynne took the pictures while Lilly looked on in shock. She was not the only one who was surprised that Dad had gotten remarried so fast.

As I watched the wedding ceremony, I remembered the entry in Dad's journal that Conny had told me about: the dream he had had about a dark-haired woman. I watched Cheri at the front of the church, the dark-haired woman who had entered our life. Suddenly, a sneaking suspicion entered my mind, a dark thought that made me wonder something terrible. Did Dad do it on purpose? Did he let Mom die? Did he let her go because Cheri was the dark-haired woman of his dreams that he thought he was meant to be with?

Eight

God talked to Cheri a lot. Almost immediately after the marriage, Cheri announced that God told her she should change her kids' names. Tom became Timothy, Emily became Beth, and Allen became Adam. I thought it was weird, but the new Timothy, Beth, and Adam did not seem to mind. They took it all in stride, probably because they were used to Cheri doing things like that.

Years later, I found out that right after the marriage, she even made Dad sign papers that if he did not want to be religious anymore, or if the marriage did not work out, that she would get custody of Jon, Rebekah, and me.

Cheri said the name changes were symbolic of new beginnings: our new life together and new beginning with God. We would start our new life in a new home. That was something else that God told Cheri we should do. It was another part of all of us starting down a new path together. At least, that is what Cheri said. I think they wanted to move out because there were too many memories of Mom around, and Cheri was trying her best to erase Mom from our minds.

I was not ready yet, hoping perhaps I might get another glimpse of Mom in the laundry room. That stuff about God and new beginnings was just a convenient story.

We were going to rent a furnished house in Cedar Rapids. That is where God told Cheri we should go. God also said that we should give all of our stuff away, which I thought was rather opportune, because we could not afford a moving truck anyway. All our furniture stayed behind for the Christian missionaries that were taking over our house, and our excess belongings were donated. But by that point, I did not have many extras to donate anyway. Everything I owned that had had value to me had already been taken away or burned.

It was harder on Jon to give his stuff away. He had a little mo-ped and go-cart that he had bought with his savings. But God did not seem to care about that because they, too, had to be given away. Jon did not complain or protest or ask why, like I would have. He was quiet and kept everything inside and did what he was told.

I was the one who was different. I was the odd one out, the one who did not like Cheri and did not accept her, regardless of her attempts to win me over in the beginning. She got under my skin. When I was in the same room with her, the tension in the air was thick. I had always been close to Dad. My relationship with Dad threatened Cheri. She did not like to think that I was daddy's girl. If I had a question or problem, I always went to Dad, not her, for the answer.

Before Mom died, she and I were not super close, but I had been getting closer to her at the end of her life by helping her out more in the kitchen with daily household chores. She had been teaching me how to can tomatoes that last month, which was tedious and took all day. I soon forgot how to can tomatoes, but the memory and the time shared with her stayed with me, preciously in my heart. Cheri could not replace my real Mom so easily, even though she desperately wanted too. She wanted me to call her Mom, but I could not.

We moved out of the Center Point house in February. As we pulled away from the house, I looked back at it one more time, trying to keep a mental picture of it in my head. I did not know if I would ever see it again. The carpet was dingy and the curtains outdated and nothing in it was nice, but it was the last place I had seen Mom, and there were memories of her in every room. In our new place, there would not be anything to remind me of Mom. From then on, I would have to carry her in my heart, just like Cheri had said.

The rent for the new house we moved into was paid for with Dad's labor. He was going to fix up the downstairs bathroom, and in exchange, we could live there for a while, until something else in the house needed fixing up, or until we got kicked out and had to find a new place. Dad and Cheri did not seem worried about it. God would provide.

I was expecting the new house to be just as old and shabby as the one we had just left, but it was a step up—a couple steps up even. It was relatively new, a beautiful split-level with five tiny bedrooms. As I explored the rooms, I began to feel something I had not felt in a long time: excitement. This was a house I would not feel embarrassed bringing friends to, not that I had any. Maybe the new beginnings Cheri was talking about would mean new friends as well.

My bedroom was upstairs, right next to Dad and Cheri's. It was small but quaint, big enough for a bed and dresser. It was easier to keep an eye on me that way. I was singled out and constantly watched. I told myself that at least I had my own room, something I had never had before. But if I thought that things were going to get better, I was wrong. Life seemed to go only one way in our household: for the worse.

Cheri and Dad became even more strict with us. It started out with having to mute the commercials when we were watching television. Shows like Gentle Ben, Grizzly Adams, and Little House on the Prairie were a select few that we were allowed to watch. Then, we were not allowed to watch any TV at all except public television and the news. Since we did not have cable, that was really all the antenna could pick up anyway. Listening to the radio got extremely hard too. Soon, we could not listen even to

Christian radio anymore. Any type of radio station was considered too worldly and strictly forbidden. The only kind of music we were allowed to hear was Christian music on tapes that Cheri and Dad made personally.

I did not like these new rules. Being fourteen, I was constantly trying to assert my independence. Soon after moving into the house, I discovered the room under the stairs. It was a treasure trove of everything forbidden to us. I found magazines — even dirty ones — VHS tapes of movies we were not allowed to watch, and even an old radio.

I tucked the radio under my shirt and quietly snuck it upstairs to my bedroom. I promptly hid it underneath the bed where there was an outlet I could plug it into. At night, when the lights were off and everything was quiet, I crawled under the bed and turned the radio on, keeping the volume just low enough that I could hear it but not too loud for Dad and Cheri to hear.

Michael Jackson and Madonna were sweet music to my ears after hearing so many Christian songs for so long. It was my salvation, at least for the next week. I should have known it would not last for long. Nothing good seemed to last for long in our house.

One night, when I crawled under the bed as usual, I was devastated to see the radio was gone, probably from one of Cheri's rounds of snooping through my things. And sure enough,

I was ready for the confrontation that came the next day.

"Where did you find this?" Cheri greeted me the next morning in a defiant stance at my doorway. She held the radio up like it was a skunk.

I did not want to tell her where I really found it. If I told them about the room under the stairs, they would clear it out for sure, and I was not finished exploring it yet. I was surprised they had not discovered it for themselves, but the day would come when they would. I wanted to see what other treasures I could find.

"I just found it," I said, shrugging my shoulders as if it were no big deal. I hoped she would not press me about it, but she did.

"Where did you find it?" she challenged.

"Around," I replied, scrambling to come up with a place. "In the garage," I added. That seemed a likely story.

Cheri eyeballed me as if she was not sure she should buy it. "Why were you listening to it?" she demanded.

"I don't know," I replied. I had learned that that was the safest answer to give. I could not tell her the real reasons: I was sick of the Christian music and wanted to hear real rock n' roll and be like any other teenager. I wanted to say that, but I would have been lucky if they had ever let me out of my room after that.

Cheri had already been watching me

closer since I had refused to call her Mom. I was a challenge for her almost daily, and it was becoming increasingly hard to even see her as a friend since we argued all the time. I felt she was trying to get me into trouble, to pull mine and Dad's relationship apart
and get Dad on her side. So far, it was working in her favor pretty well; I was constantly in trouble.

"This type of music is evil," Cheri said, holding the radio up and shaking it. She reminded me of a preacher standing on a pulpit, all fired up and frenzied about the wicked ways of the world. "You can't be listening to worldly music," she continued. "And I think your older brothers and sisters have been having too much of a negative influence on you. That's going to stop."

I did not know what her threat meant, but I quickly discovered I was not allowed to talk to them anymore. Before the radio incident, I had been able to speak with them on the phone once a week or so and even see them once in a great while. But all that stopped. No more contact with them.

It was not like when Mom was around, letting me sneak calls to them. Cheri and Dad really cracked down. So not only was Mom taken away from me, but my brothers and sisters were too. Now all I had left were Jon and Rebekah. But I could not look up to them, could not copy their fashion and style and aspire to be like them. I felt like I had no one. Dad and Cheri told me repeatedly that I needed to be a good example for the younger brothers and sisters.

The radio disappeared, but I still had the storage room under the stairs. Timothy and I liked to snoop around in it whenever we could get the chance, which usually meant when Dad and Cheri were praying or doing their Bible study. We always took a flashlight with us and picked through the cardboard boxes of goodies. Timothy liked to look at the magazines, especially the ones with scantily-clad women on the front. I had never heard of these type before, but every one of them had a alluring woman on the front.

Of course, our trips under the stairs did not last for long. Beth soon discovered what we were doing, and when she found our secret about the magazines, she promptly informed Dad and Cheri who just as promptly removed our gold mine. Our days under the stairs were done. Of course, I was in trouble again for this incident, not Timothy, and sent to my room to pray. I was getting rather sick of this and wondered to myself what life would be like in a normal family.

Life continued pretty much this way. Christian music, Christian friends, and Christian church on Sundays. One Sunday, we were in church, dressed in our Sunday best, listening to the preacher. It was just like every other Sunday, except that in the middle of the sermon,

Dad suddenly stood up and started preaching too, drowning out the sounds of the preacher who was behind the pulpit.

"You are not speaking God's words," he shouted, pointing at the preacher in the front.

Everyone stared at us, and I felt horribly embarrassed as Dad quoted verses from the Bible. I glanced over at Cheri. She did not look surprised, and I wondered how long they had been plotting this.

I squirmed and fidgeted in my seat, my face turning red hot from everyone staring at us. I tried to slump down in my seat so as not to be noticed, and I looked at the ground, shaking my head in disbelief. There went my chance of any new Christian friends.

"We're going to have to ask you to leave," a man said, coming over to our bench and escorting us up and out the back. They practically had to drag Dad out, who was ranting and raving at the top of his lungs about God and evil the whole time.

"We just could not be there anymore," Cheri explained when we were all outside. "They weren't following in the teachings of God."

I did not know how a church could not be following the teachings of God, but Dad and Cheri seemed glad, proud even, like they had accomplished something great.

I was surprised by it all, but secretly I thought it was kind of cool to be kicked out of church. It might be something I could tell the other kids at school and raise my self-esteem a bit. Besides, I was glad I would not have to wear the ugly long dresses to church anymore. The dresses were itchy and uncomfortable. After that, we did the home meetings again, just the eight of us, listening to Dad and Cheri preach in the living room every morning from the Bible. It was boring.

At school, I was still trying to desperately fit in. I tried anything to be a part of the group and feel like I belonged. It was almost springtime again, and I decided I wanted to go out for track, hoping this would help me fit in at school. It seemed the easiest sport to join. There would not be any expensive equipment that we could not afford to purchase; all I needed were my legs. It seemed easy enough to do. I dreamed of winning races and making new friends and being popular. Track would be my ticket in.

I practically skipped home from school with a spring in my step, the track registration papers in my hand. I thought of every possible reason that Dad and Cheri would not let me join. They could say it was evil, or too worldly, or not of God, but I would insist that they point out in the Bible where it said I could not join track.

I had other points I was ready to bring up too, like how it would allow me to meet new people and teach them about Christian ways.

Dad and Cheri were big on being missionaries and talking about God to others. Not that I would ever do it, but if it allowed me to be in track, then so be it.

I showed Dad the papers as soon as I got home. He looked over them carefully. "This is something you really want to do?" he asked, peering at me over the registration sheet. I nodded, silently praying that he would sign it. "It says here you need to get a physical in order to join," he continued.

I had not thought about that, and getting a physical meant going to the doctor. Dad did not believe in doctors, and I had not had a physical before; I was not even really sure what they were. I felt my heart sinking in my chest. I expected arguments about God and evil, not doctors.

"I want you to pray about it," Dad said, "and if you really want to, then you can sign up." I was hopeful for a moment—one brief, sweet moment. But the next second Dad added, "You'll have to pay for the doctor yourself, though."

All my hopes were gone. I did not have any money and had no way to earn money either. Dad had used the one reason that I could not argue against. It always seemed to come down to God or money. This time it was money. But, I think it was a convenient way for Dad to put the blame on something else, so that I would not put the blame on him. After all, it was not he who was forbidding me to join. It was me having no money that was to blame.

If track was not going to work, then I had other ideas of how I could fit in. I had been hiding a swimsuit from Cheri, one I got from Lynne and Lilly. They stopped by the house once shortly after we moved in, and Dad and Cheri were out getting groceries. It was before the privilege of seeing and talking to them was taken away, and I did not realize it was the last time I was going to see them for a very long time. They gave me a fashionable orange Body Glove swimsuit with stylish black lining on it. I hid it under my mattress. But as the swimming lessons in Physical Education came near, I pulled it out and put it on and admired myself in front of the mirror.

I was excited to show it off to all my classmates. I wondered what they would think of seeing me in it, when they were so used to .seeing me in plain, hand-me-down clothes. I imagined the comments they would make, telling me how cool I looked. I was so excited, I could hardly wait, my heart was doing belly flops just thinking how the other kids in school would *ooh* and *awe* over my fashionable swimsuit.

I was ecstatic the afternoon before our first day of swimming. Not only was I going to learn how to swim, but I was going to look good doing it as well.

After school, I went to my room and

closed the door tightly, then slipped into the swimsuit one last time. I did little poses like I had seen in the playboy magazines and flipped my long hair around and thought how all the girls would envy me and all the boys would admire me.

While I was prancing around the room in my swimsuit, I heard some scratches at the door. It was opened just a crack, but I thought I had shut it all the way. I was not sure if I saw someone. I quickly stripped the swimsuit off and threw it in the dresser and scrambled back into my regular clothes, praying that no one had seen me. I poked my head out into the hallway to find it empty. I sat on my bed nervously and pulled out some homework, deciding if anyone came to check on me, it would make me look innocent. I stayed in my room until Cheri announced supper was ready.

We gathered at the table, but as soon as we all sit down, Cheri got up and disappeared down the hall. She came marching back to the kitchen, and my face turned beet red to see what she held in her hand. It was my swimsuit.

"Where did you get this?" she asked in her loud, demanding voice.

I looked around at the others, wondering which one had betrayed me. But none of them looked guilty. All their eyes were fixed on me and Cheri, wondering what was going to happen.

"Where did you get it?" she firmly asked

again.

"I found it," I replied, rather embarrassed, hoping she would believe it. After all, I had found the radio.

"This is too new to be something you found," she said. "So where did you get it?" She knew full well that I had no money and no way to buy it.

I looked around, stalling, hoping to come up with a better answer, but nothing came to me. The truth was the only way out. "The Twins gave it to me a while ago," I finally retorted, my face now burnt red, and my palms were sweaty.

"Your sisters," Cheri snorted. "I should have known as much. They're a bad influence on you. I should have forbidden you from seeing them long ago."

She held the swimsuit away from her at arm's length, as if afraid she would burst into flames if it touched her. "This is way too sexy for a girl of fourteen. This is too sexy for a woman of any age. You'll not be wearing it."

"I'm not wearing some old-fashioned thing," I protested. "The only way I'm taking swimming is if I can wear something stylish."

I was surprised at myself for confronting Cheri, but I wanted that swimsuit. I had dreamed of wearing it, and I was not going to give up on it so easily. I figured they had to let me participate in gym class, and if I was going to participate, I needed a suit. But Cheri already had that taken care of.

"Style doesn't matter to God," Cheri replied. "All that matters is obeying your parents and doing what you're told."

And with that she went into her bedroom. When she came back my swimsuit was gone, and there was another one in her hand: an old, ugly one, loose and bunchy, probably from the 1960's, with a skirt that was decorated with red and purple zig-zag stripes. I laughed when I saw it.

"I am not wearing that. Are you kidding?" I scoffed. "I'm not going to go to swim practice."

"Suit yourself," Cheri said. "This is a perfectly fine swimsuit. If you don't want to learn how to swim, that's your choice."

I was mad at Cheri, madder than I had ever been. It would have been easier to take if I had at least been able to go to one swim practice wearing the cool Body Glove swimsuit. All my dreams and fantasies were over. I was so looking forward to it and all the kids noticing me. I quickly got up from the table and rushed to my room, slamming the door loudly behind me.

The next day, during gym class, I sit on the bench next to the pool wearing all of my clothes. When the other kids asked why I was not swimming, I told them I was afraid I would drown.

I felt like I was drowning already.

Nine

One May evening, over a dinner of what I liked to call sloppy, bland goulash — hamburger, tomato, and noodles — Cheri and Dad announced that we were moving to Texas. Cheri's sister, Kim, lived in Texas with her husband, and we were supposedly moving to get Kim right with God. But Kim's marriage to a rich Texaco Oil tycoon was troubled, and Cheri wanted to help Kim get as much as she could out of the divorce.

It was another move in only a matter of months. We had just gotten used to living in our new place in Cedar Rapids and already we were leaving it. I was not sad this time, like I was leaving the Center Point house. I was looking forward to it. I had never been out of Iowa before, except to go to visit relatives in Minnesota a few times. Texas was new territory with me, a new world to discover, and I was excited to explore it. I hoped again that things would be better in Texas, but I should have known better. They never got better, only worse.

By the weekend, we were quietly gone. No family members were to know we had left. Our few belongings, clothes mostly, were packed into the old station wagon. We drove all day and did not stop until we reached Oklahoma.

Dad pulled into a run-down motel off the highway, and we all crammed into a tiny room with two beds. Dad and Cheri had told the management that there were only two adults and two kids, which I did not understand how lying fit in with their religious view.

The youngest ones had to sleep on the floor. Dad and Cheri occupied one bed while we four older kids squeezed together like sardines into the other. It was a sleepless night for me, not just because Jon's feet were in my face all night, but because I was itching to see Texas.

After another long day of driving, we arrived in Montgomery, Texas, our new home. I was surprised we had a house to stay in already, with furniture no less, probably purchased for us with Kim's money since we did not have any of our own. I had a feeling Dad, Cheri and Kim had been planning our move for a while, and it had not been as impromptu as it seemed.

Our new house was not as nice as the one we had just left. It was certainly smaller. There were only two bedrooms, so Dad and Cheri got the master bedroom and the three girls — Beth, Rebekah, and I — shared the other. The boys had a makeshift bedroom in the attic. There were no stairs to go up, just a ladder that led to a hole in the ceiling. It was hot up there in the summer, and Jon and Adam had to share a bunkbed. I felt sorry for them.

Texas was not so bad at first. We got to spend a lot of time at Kim's house — which was truly a mansion — while Cheri and Dad did Bible study with Kim. Sometimes we were dropped off and got to spend the night or the entire weekend.

Being at Kim's was like being at an amusement park. Her kids had TVs and computers and video games in their rooms, and we spent a lot of our time playing Play Station or watching television programs we would never be allowed to watch at home. All six of us kids wanted to play, so we took turns while one of us stood guard at the door.

Cheri and Dad were too busy with the Bible to check up on us, and when we stayed overnight, Kim did not know any better than to let us watch what we wanted and play what we wanted. Also there were all kinds of candy and treats that Kim provided for us kids when we stayed. "Eat as much as you want," she would say, happy to entertain us in her big fancy house.

I had played video games before at friends' houses, mainly Super Mario Brothers and Atari. But the Play Station was something new, the games were more violent, not shooting fireballs at cartoon mushrooms, but shooting guns and playing war. Still, it was exciting to play because it was something to do. It was something different and out of the ordinary from our daily lives.

We all knew we were not supposed to, but we did not care. And I, especially, felt a little triumph inside me when I played, knowing I was breaking Cheri's and Dad's rules, knowing that for that brief time, they could not control me. Of course, that did not last for long.

Cheri and Dad caught on to what we were doing, and soon Kim knew better as well. The time they spent preaching to her was starting to sink in, and Kim was, day by day, starting to become more like her religious sister.

After that, we ended up going swimming in the outdoor pool a lot. We would play Marco Polo and Catch Me If You Can all day long, our skin becoming red and sun burnt at the day's end. It was so much fun. It was a nice break from our simple, boring, small house in the woods.

The pool at Kim's house inspired us. We decided that we wanted a pool as well. So we asked Cheri and Dad if we could have one. I was not really expecting them to say yes. After all, I did not think we would be able to afford one. But I had forgotten, we had Kim in our lives now. So we were allowed to get one under one condition: we had to dig the hole for the pool. They said if we dug the hole, God would provide for the rest, and God did provide—with Kim's money.

The six of us kids, armed with shovels, dug a hole in the backyard. We worked on it almost every day for about a month, but it felt like it took a year. I spent more time digging than anybody else. I loved the physical labor. It kept me busy when I usually was bored in the afternoons. As soon as I got done with my homeschooling studies, I grabbed a shovel and headed for the backyard hole.

Every shovel of dirt had to be carefully shoveled out of the hole and spread out somewhere else in the yard. We had lots of low spots in the yard that Dad wanted filled in. We made mounds for flower beds in the yard, kind of like a nice landscape pattern. The pool was shaped like an angel, with a large round head that was supposed to be a hot tub, and the pool part shaped like wings.

Once the hole was dug, Dad and Cheri hired some Mexican men to come out and pour the concrete for the pool. We got a diving board for it and even bought a slide at a garage sale. It was fun for the first few weeks of that summer, but soon the novelty was gone.

In Texas, Dad started doing his casting out of devils and demons again, but it was not like what he did around the time I was born.

"There are demons all around," he said, "constantly trying to tempt us and take over our bodies."

And it seemed, of everyone in the house, the demons were most trying to take over me. Dad was constantly laying his hands on me, trying to cast the demons out. I was just a teenaged girl at that time, trying to fit in and feel normal, but everything I did and every time I rebelled just meant to Dad and Cheri that I had demons trying to take over my body.

One of the first times Dad cast demons out of me was after I made some cookies. I liked to bake and remembered that when Mom baked, she was always experimenting and adding new things to her recipes. Up in the cupboard, I found some rum extract, and I added it to the cookie recipe. I was so proud when I presented them at dinner, thinking how I was starting to be just like Mom.

Cheri quickly put an end to my happy thoughts. She took one bite of the cookie and spit it out, saying, "What did you do to these cookies?"

"Nothing," I replied innocently, thinking that I had not done anything wrong.

"Look at me," she ordered, "look at my eyes." I did what I was told, seeing the way her eyes seemed to look right into my soul as she glared at me. It was almost an evil glare, and her eyes practically wanted to pop out of her head. It was hard to look at her when she stared at me like that. But every time I got into trouble, she gave me that look, and I had a hard time meeting people's eyes after that.

"I just added some rum extract to them to give them a little bit of flavor." I had tried the cookies myself and did not think that they tasted that bad, actually sweeter with a fruity hint to them.

"You added rum to the cookies?" Cheri asked, incredulous. "Are you trying to get us all drunk?" She took the platter of cookies and threw them in the garbage. "You wasted perfectly good expensive ingredients. What's gotten into you?"

"The Devil," Dad said, before I could reply.

"Demons," Cheri agreed, nodding her head. "You have the sin of alcoholism in you."

I did not think that any of it was such a big deal. I did not understand how experimenting with a bit of rum extract in the cookie dough meant I had the sin of alcoholism in me. And now they thought demons were trying to possess me, and they had to cast them out.

"I can see the demon right now," Dad said, "taking the form of a monkey. It's on your back."

And the next thing I knew, Dad was leading me over to the couch. He sat me down, put his hands on me, and started to pray over me. "I rebuke you in the name of Jesus," Dad said, closing his eyes and putting one of his hands on my head.

He shouted out Bible verses over my head for at least half an hour before he announced that the demon had left. I thought it was all ridiculous silliness, but Dad and Cheri began to insist I had a demon on me every time I did something wrong in their eyes, which was almost daily.

I began having to endure casting out sessions every day it seemed, sometimes lasting up to an hour while they put their hands on me and prayed over me. I would just sit there in quiet defiance, for if I complained or disagreed, the praying and laying on of hands session would last even longer until I gave in and humbly agreed with what they were doing over me.

Dad said I had a choice to choose God or the demon in me which happened to be the monkey on my back at that moment; I did not feel that I had a choice; it was Cheri's way or else be in trouble all the time. I usually gave in, tired and hungry from sitting still and being prayed over for what seemed all afternoon. I just felt like Cheri was picking on me all the time and getting Dad more on her side with each incident that occurred.

The way I felt, they could have just locked me in my room forever. I was beginning to loathe the secluded new lifestyle we seemed to be living with the homeschooling and no outside friends. Cheri made it clear that my brothers and sisters were my only friends. I did not understand how I was to act my age, or grow and mature as a young teen, if I did not have any friends my age.

I was feeling trapped and imprisoned. It was a helpless, hopeless feeling that I could not seem to overcome. I had had a small taste of freedom when I spent time with my Christian friend, Sharon, before and after school the year prior, and boy was it hard to take two steps backward.

"You need to start talking to God," Dad instructed me. "You need to pray more. That will keep the demons away."

I spent quiet time in my room, trying very hard to hear God's voice inside of me when I prayed, but I did not know what God's voice was supposed to sound like. Nothing ever seemed to happen. I grew impatient and weary of saying prayers and listening, longing for a response, a noise, just some type of answer, but nothing ever happened. There was always just a long silence.

I wondered what was wrong. How did Dad and Cheri hear God's voice every day, even about the little things, like what clothes to wear, but I never heard anything. I did not think I was a bad person. I did not usually try to do things that would get me into trouble, and if I did do something wrong, I always repented and asked God for forgiveness.

"I try to hear God talk to me," I said to dad, "but I never hear anything, and I've tried and tried so many times."

"God speaks to us in all kinds of ways," he replied. "Sometimes dreams, or visions, or speaking in tongues. It's not always a direct voice. Be patient and keep waiting, and in time you will hear."

So I continued to try, desperately wanting to hear God's voice inside of me, but I never heard anything. I was beginning to wonder if Dad and Cheri were really hearing from God or were they just making it up to get their way? When I was younger, I never doubted Mom and Dad — they were the adults and I believed everything they said. But I was a teenager now, and I found myself doubting that Dad and Cheri were actually hearing from God.

Daily life in Texas was starting to be a bore. Dad and Cheri did not work, since *God would provide*, which of course meant that Kim would provide. So they were around all the time — there was no getting away from them. Life started to fall into a regular routine.

When we woke up in the morning, we would gather in the living room and have our prayer meeting. It usually lasted an hour or so. We would all bring copies of our Bibles, and Dad would start by asking if we had a dream or vision that we wanted to share from the night before. Someone would talk about their dream, and Dad would interpret them. Then we all opened our Bibles, and Dad would pick a section for us to follow along with as he read it. If someone was not feeling well — usually Cheri — we would lay hands on the person and pray over them. Then we ate breakfast.

When we moved to Texas, we did not get to go to public school anymore. We were homeschooled. The Christian A-Beka curriculum was popular in Texas, and that is what we used. We spent from breakfast to lunch reading and answering questions, taking quizzes and tests.

I missed being at a regular public school. I did not like never having interaction with anyone in the outside world. I wanted friends but was not allowed to have any—not even Christian friends anymore.

There was a girl I met in the neighborhood shortly after we moved to Texas, but Dad and Cheri would not let me be friends with her, even though she was a Christian.

"Your brothers and sisters are your friends now," she told me. But I was tired of having only my family to interact with and desperately wanted to have contact with the outside world.

After lunch we did our hobbies. All of us were required by Dad and Cheri to have a hobby. I had a couple of different ones. I took a Spanish course on the computer, and I would learn one hundred vocabulary words a day, but by the next day, I would forget them all, because I did not have any
one to talk to. I also did woodworking.

Kim had gotten us a lathe and a scroll saw and some other materials. We would get scraps of wood, and I would work out in the carport. Jon and I would spend a couple hours out there every afternoon.

I made stagecoaches or covered wagons or model T cars. I liked to make intricate, detailed designs. I used twigs for spokes in the wheels, so they could turn, or I made hidden compartments in the cars. Most of the items we made became gifts for holidays or birthdays since we could not afford to buy any fancy stuff. It was strange, but sometimes it felt nice to give a homemade gift rather than a store-bought one.

Sometimes, in the afternoon, we played games with each other. We had a badminton net at the side of the house. We liked to see how long we could keep the badminton birdie up in the air.

We also played croquet, swam in the pool, or even went fishing at the nearby pond. After supper, we would all gather around the television and watch the news, since Dad thought it was important that we knew what was happening in the world. Then we watched old movies on VHS tapes. Dad loved John Wayne, so we watched a lot of old westerns.

We also watched shows on public television like *Wild America* or *Nature*, and we could watch movies like *The Sound of Music* or *Swiss Family Robinson*. I ended up hating *The Sound of Music* because we watched it thousands of times. It got to the point where I was so sick of watching it, I had every song memorized by heart, and not because I wanted to either.

When we moved to Texas, Cheri began to assert her authority over the family more and more. One particular incident marked the beginning of her rule. We all gathered for supper, and we sat down at the table to eat. We said our prayers and were picking up our forks when Cheri suddenly looked at Dad and announced, "No, you are submissive to me now. I am going to be the one hearing God's word, and you will listen and humble yourself to me."

Dad put his fork down and said, "When you tell me that God says it's time for me to eat, then I will start eating."

The rest of us started eating, and I glanced around at the others, trying to see what they were thinking, but they hid their reactions. I then believed that Cheri was even weirder than before, and I disliked her even more for what she was doing to Dad. But Dad did not seem to mind, and that bothered me too.

After a couple of minutes, Cheri said, "You can start eating now." Dad picked up his fork and took a bite of his food as if nothing out of the ordinary had happened.

That incident started a new precedent in our house. After that, Dad waited for Cheri to give the okay for everything he did. He started going to her instead of to God for decisions, because God was speaking through her now. To me, it all seemed like a control game, and Cheri was playing God. Dad was her puppet, and she was pulling his strings. Soon, we kids would follow in his path like the blind leading the blind, except I could see just fine. Cheri was becoming my enemy, a controlling, conniving stepmom.

Ten

Bulimia was the next phase of my life. Lilly showed me how to do it once. When the stepmom started to feed me extra food, to fatten me up, I tried to sneak it to the dog, or I would eat it but get rid of it later. I would eat the extra food she gave me, but I would purge it later. It was not because I thought I was fat; it became a control thing for me. Cheri wanted me to eat the fat from the meat, but I would also try to sneak it to the dog.

In Texas, I started to purge almost regularly. They thought I was getting too skinny and needed to gain weight. The other girls had gained weight. Lilly told me how she got rid of food. So, I thought if I had to be force fed, then I would get rid of my food also. I felt like I was starting to get extra big portions, and I would not want seconds because I was full, but Cheri would give me seconds anyway. I was not allowed to leave the table until I had finished.

Usually, I only did this at dinner time, because it was only at dinner I had to eat so much. Breakfast and lunch were such small meals, I would not want to purge later. But still, at breakfast, Cheri tried to give me extra butter on my toast, so much that sometimes it was saturated. I tried to pitch it under the table to Charles, our dog. He would sit by me, hungrily licking his chops until Cheri caught on to what was happening.

We found Charles walking around the streets in Houston on a recent trip to Aunt Kim's home. He was mangy with long, curly hair all matted over his eyes. Someone had abandoned him on the side of the road. It was hard for Dad to say no to our pleas to keep him, so Cheri named him Charles Purem or Charles for short. Cheri said God spoke to her, and Purem meant he was pure of heart in God's eyes. So, it was okay for us kids to keep him.

Charles was a male cocker spaniel. However, until I washed and brushed him, he looked like a shaggy mutt. He loved playing chase with me in the fenced yard in front. I adored brushing out his tight, soft curls after bathing him. He always seemed to be rolling in the mud, so it took a good amount of time cleaning and drying him. I did not mind, it passed the boring afternoons when I had nothing else to do but read my Bible.

If Charles was not around to sneak scraps of food to, I would put it in my pockets and throw it away later. They eventually caught on, and I was not allowed to leave the table until I finished my food. Then later, I remembered what Lilly had told me, and I started to deliberately throw it back up.

There was a walking space behind the

makeshift greenhouse Dad made for Cheri in the backyard, and it was next to the fence. There were tall weeds back there. The ground was sandy so it was easy to dig, and I would go back there and dig a hole and throw up, then bury it, but only if the bathroom was occupied or too many people were around.

I turned the fan on in the bathroom so no one could hear me. Sometimes I would wait a bit until we went to bed because I did not get the chance earlier. I would sneak out of the bedroom and go to the boy's bathroom on the far side of the house.

I would wear extra baggy clothes so they could not tell if I was gaining weight or not.

If I had to wait too long, more of the acid would come up and not as much food would come out. It got easier to do over time, and I got better at it.

It was easier to know what foods to eat to help it come up quicker. Creamy saucy foods like yogurt, ice cream, and milk would make it all come up easier. Pizza and breads were hard to bring up because they got doughy. I felt like it got stuck in my throat, and I had a harder time bringing it up, it took more effort. It took five to ten minutes total every time. It took longer at first, but I got better at it as I did it more often. Soon it was second nature.

Sometimes I cut my throat or scratched it with my fingernail, and it would be sore for a couple days until it healed. After that, I always made sure my nails were kept short.

I never threw up sweets, which did not make any sense. If we got a treat during the day, I would save it. Something like powdered mini donuts, I would keep in my pocket and save for later. In the evening, when I threw up, I would get hungry again. But I never threw up sweets. The main reason I threw up was because I did not want Cheri to control what I ate. Sometimes, I had sweet food in my pocket, and by evening, it would be a crumbled mess, but I ate it anyway, pocket lint and thread strings and all.

Kim had candy jars, and I would take handfuls of candy and save it for later. Since I would be hungry again after expelling dinner, I would eat some candy when my stomach growled. Even a small piece of candy would relieve the emptiness in my stomach.

I felt like I had the upper hand, like Cheri did not have control. This was one thing I could control, and she did not know it though she always wanted to know everything. I felt proud, knowing she really could not control me. I was not thinking so much about my health or wellness when my throat got sore and scratched after throwing up. There was a sense of pride from winning the battle I had with Cheri. If she wanted to fatten me up, then she had another think coming. I thought to myself, "Let the games begin!"

My body was mine and no one, especially

my stepmom, could make me plump. This was the one thing I did have control over, and she was steaming mad about it. I could see it every time I looked into her eyes when she told me to eat more. Her piercing, glaring, evil eyeballs popped out at me every time she told me what and how much to eat. I just shuddered, thinking about it.

I do not think I ever would have had a problem if Cheri would have just left me alone and not tried to give me extra food portions or fat scraps from meat. I do not blame her at all for my eating disorder. That I did of my own free will after learning how to do it from my older sister. Because of my stepmother forcing extra food on me, I ended up in a downward spiral. It was bulimia, and it got out of control as time went on.

I felt so deflated and stepped on in my heart, like my free-will had been robbed from me. Sometimes I felt like Cheri and Dad's robot. My eating disorder was the only form of control I had left. They had stripped me of all my teenage freedoms, and this was the one last thing they could not take from me or control. In a way, I embraced my bulimia like a hidden treasure.

One day, a UPS guy came to the door and he had huge leg muscles and arm muscles. I could not stop staring at him. I asked him how he got muscles like that. He told me he worked out a lot. I decided I wanted to be muscular too, so I jumped rope and hula hooped, since I had no other way to workout. I did it every day, setting goals for myself to see how long I could do it.

Soon Dad caught me. I was out in the carport, and Dad wanted to know what I was doing. I told him about the UPS guy, and I showed him my muscle. He told me that that was a sin. It was not Christian. It was not womanly, and it was obsessive. He said I had to stop this.

So after that, I started to sneak in my exercises. If Dad was doing a prayer meeting or doing schoolwork with the kids, I would sneak off and exercise. In the pool, I would kick my legs or do pushups on the edge. Or, inside behind my locked bedroom door, I did sit ups and pushups in bed.

I wore a belt to bed. Under my pajamas, I wore a fabric belt. I would strap it snug so it was almost pinching and hurting. I thought that if it was kept tight it would make my waist smaller. I was obsessed with trying to stay thin. I would not overeat. I also chopped wood because I knew that was good exercise.

Sometimes I would spend a whole hot, sweaty afternoon chopping a cord of firewood. I secretly checked later that night, flexing my bicep muscle to see if it had grown any bigger. Either the light in the closet was not bright enough or my muscles had not grown significantly.

Rebekah was seven years younger than me. She was naive and enslaved by our religious upbringing. Jon was three years younger than me. Jon liked to help Dad a lot. He helped Dad with his carpentry, handing him tools and fetching his supplies. Jon was the quiet, shy one. He liked to take computers or radios apart and carefully put them back together. I would hurt his feelings and not realize it. This resulted in him being up in his room crying and upset. Then I would get into trouble.

I never did it on purpose, but Dad always reprimanded me. I just spoke my mind, without thinking it might hurt someone else's feelings. I wore my heart on my sleeve.

Jon seemed to go along with Cheri's religious thinking and lifestyle. He never put up a fuss, because he saw how much I got into trouble for it. I frequently was sent to my room to pray, and I did not want any part of that anymore. Jon never talked back and did as he was told.

Eleven

We could not go anywhere by ourselves. We all had to do everything together, even trips to the grocery store. I just wanted to stay home, but I was not allowed. God wanted us all to go together. Nobody ever stayed home alone. If one went for a walk, we would all go. If one wanted to go swimming in the lake nearby, we all had to go.

I did not want to go to the grocery store. Sometimes I would ask to stay in the car, and they would let me. I would look at other families laughing or talking to their kids, and I wondered what a normal family would be like. I wondered if I would ever live in a normal family. I longed to be in a normal family. I wished we could be normal.

After about two years in Texas, Conny and her husband Steve came for a visit. Conny and Steve were living in Texas, and I did not even know they were that close to us. They showed up in a big red Toyota in the middle of the morning when we were doing our school work.

Someone asked, "Who's that?"

We all got up and went out. We were excited because we had visitors. It was something different breaking up the monotony of the day.

I recognized Conny at once. I had never met Steve, so I did not know who he was. Conny said, "Hi, my husband and I were in the area and thought we'd stop by."

Dad and Cheri were shocked and surprised. Later, after I had moved out, Conny told me she had a hard time finding us. She did not know where we had gone since we had left Iowa. All of her letters and Christmas cards addressed to me had been returned. After a lengthy search on her computer, she located where we were living in Texas and could not believe we had been living so close to her all this time.

She and new husband, Steve, had relocated to Texas for work shortly after we also moved to Texas. Dad and Cheri purposely moved us to Texas quietly, careful to not leave any bread crumbs behind so no relatives could track us down and possibly remove us kids from our secret, religious environment. I desperately wished an older brother or sister, aunt or uncle, would have come to my rescue and taken me away. Sadly, I did not know how to contact them and was afraid of getting into trouble with Cheri or Dad. They were keeping a very close eye on me as of late.

Dad and Cheri told us to go back to our rooms. I obeyed, following Rebekah back inside the front door. In my heart, I was dying to talk to my sister. I was afraid that I might not get a chance, if Cheri had a say in it. They were outside for a while talking, and then they all came into the house. Dad and Cheri sat down in the living room and started praying for them, talking about Scriptures. Dad said Conny had a monkey on her back, and she needed to be prayed over, because he believed there were demonic powers at work.

While they were still inside, I went outside to play at the side of the house where I could make out what they were saying through the window, because I was curious to know what they were talking about. It was religious stuff about how God wanted us to be one big family. Dad and Cheri wanted them to come live with us and be one big happy family and get right with God.

I went back in, and Dad had his hands on Conny's head. They stayed about two to three hours total, then said they had to go. I did not get a chance to talk to Conny, because Dad and Cheri kept too close of an eye on me. I was so sad.

I was horrendously upset that I missed any chance to possibly talk to Conny. I wanted to talk to her so badly and ask her to take me out of this horribly religious hell hole, but the chance never came. I knew Cheri made it nearly impossible for this to happen. I was pretty afraid of Cheri by then, by the way her eyes always glared at me, the way she seemed so evil.

We were told that our natural family members was not of God, and if anyone else came around, we were not to get close to them. We were strictly ordered to stay hidden in our rooms and pretend we were not there. Cheri said there were worldly and unclean evil spirits around them.

Because I could hear them being preached to the entire time, I was very upset. I forced my bedroom window open and slithered outside and chopped wood because I was so mad. I did not understand what was wrong with them. Why could I not see them? They got completely fed up, and they left.

Then Cheri bellowed, "Your sister is like a witch. She is in rebellion to God, which is the same as the sin of witchcraft."

I did not understand why Conny was not considered a good person. She seemed so normal to me when they visited. She was far from witchy, whatever that meant. She seemed awesome to me.

The fear of Cheri shouting at us kids made everyone uneasy. No one wanted to see Cheri upset, because she would get her Bible out and blurt God's words to us and none of us liked that.

We all grudgingly went to our rooms to leave Dad and Cheri alone to talk to each other about the trouble Conny and Steve brought to our home. Since they discovered us living in Texas, more family members might come and

Cheri did not want that. She was mad; you could see it in her eyes.

After Conny and Steve's visit, Cheri thought we should get away for a while. She decided God wanted us to go on a trip to Houston. We went grocery shopping at a big surplus warehouse. We encountered a large dumpster that appeared to be full of computer equipment.

My brother, Timothy, asked Cheri if it would be okay if we went back and checked out the stuff because it might be salvageable. Surprisingly, Cheri said it was okay, so we went back and grabbed some of the best of the bunch. We took the components home where Timothy and Jon managed to bring most of it back to life. It was amazing; we each had our own computer. We had no internet, but I had a Spanish program I could learn.

We also ended up getting some cheesy games on floppy disk at a garage sale. Anything was better than what we had before, which was nothing.

Most of what we were allowed to watch was old musicals, *John Wayne* movies, and some westerns because Dad liked them. While watching these movies, I was inspired to recreate the old wagons by carving them out of wood. I looked at some woodworking books and magazines and wondered what some of those things would look like carved of wood. I went and got little scraps of wood and made a

Model T, a stage coach and a peddler's wagon. I carved lots of things out of wood.

Naturally, I could not afford to buy wood, so I got it for free at a local lumber mill. The management felt sorry for us kids. I often spent half the day doing my make-shift curriculum, and the other half whittling something out of wood. For Christmas, we always made each other handmade gifts.

Cheri would say that God wanted us to go to garage sales. I knew what that meant. We would go out and rummage through other peoples' belongings, finding lots of nice things, but, I would not get any of it. It was the same old story. I was destined to have nothing that I wanted. I was starting to just give in, realizing I would get nowhere with Cheri in charge.

Sometimes, we would stay up late at night and talk about what we wanted to do when we grew up. We girls shared a room and the boys shared a room. Beth and I always wanted to have a big family with a bunch of kids, maybe on a big farm. It was something we dreamed about, but Beth and I knew our chances were slim, the way things were going, that we would ever see any of our dreams come true.

Cheri did a lot of yelling. She would glare right into my eyes, and her spit would mist my face. I would tell her not to yell. To this day, I have a hard time looking people in the eye from these instances. It was a type of mental abuse that was belittling and hurtful.

One time, I had a Sunday dress on, and I twirled in front of the mirror, admiring my growing figure. Dad just happened to walk by and said I had the spirit of vanity in me and needed to immediately change, and pray, asking God for forgiveness. I knew they did not want me to have any fun. I did not think it was a bad thing to admire myself in the mirror. Every time I turned around, they were constantly deflating my ego.

When we kids would go bike riding, we were supposed to stay together. If we did not, then I would get into trouble because Joel would tell on me. I was the oldest, and I was supposed to set a Godly, good example for the others. But, I was tired of having the responsibility of setting the Christian example.

Another time I got into trouble was from a horribly itchy poison ivy rash that broke out all over my body. It was all over my face too. I had been picking berries in the woods with Beth. She was not allergic, so she did not have a reaction, even though we were knee deep in the poisonous plants.

I saw some weird, old bottles high up in our bathroom cabinet that were for snake bites or some such thing. They were up there when we bought the house. I was willing to try anything to stop the maddening scratchy itch on my chin and face, so I quietly snuck one of those dusty bottles down and dumped a heaping amount of this putrid, smelly liquid in my hands, wiping it on my face.

As it turned out, it was not medicine. It was some type of acid. I watched in horror as my skin turned black almost instantly. The "snake bite potion" smelled a bit like burning flesh and ate away my skin.

The itch, however, was gone, leaving a cooling sensation. My face looked horrible, so I tried to wipe the black area off, but to no avail. I was excited the itch was gone but petrified, because I knew I would be chastised once everyone saw me. There was just no way to hide the hideous sight.

I think Dad and Cheri should have taken me to a real doctor, but they did not. God was the Healer, they always would tell me, and it did not matter what my illness or injury was.

Dad and Cheri were so mad at me. They took the remaining acid away, and the black skin slowly fell off after a while, replaced by new perfect skin. I was lucky it did not leave a scar, and I never really knew what exactly that acid was since they took it away so fast.

I also did not know at that young age that doctors had specific medicine for poison ivy that would have healed and taken the itch away. Cheri told me I had done something wrong, and God was punishing me, but by this point, I was getting used to being in trouble.

I woke up every morning and put on clothes that I thought looked cool for a teenager. Dad took one look at me as I strolled leisurely into the living room and shook his head. He would point back towards my room. That meant I needed to change. The clothes Dad wanted me to wear were baggy and shapeless. God wanted us to wear plain colored clothes. I complained and protested. I was sick of all this type of clothing.

"Yuck, yuck, yuck," I grumbled under my breathe as I shuffled back slowly to my room, making a face in disgust at Beth as she smiled back in her nice newer jeans, recently purchased from a garage sale.

I was so sick of being controlled. Hot and mad, I did as I was told and put the boring, baggy clothes back on.

God did not want me to wear that, so I would have to go change, this was an almost daily routine. I was looking forward to moving out more and more. I could just tell it was going to be a while, and that drove me nuts.

Sometimes we took field trips. We went to Galveston a couple times to watch the dolphins. We would get chicken meat and put it on fish hooks and catch blue crabs. We would put them in a bucket with ice and take them home to eat. It was awesome to see the dolphins, they were beautiful. You could see them chase each other, and they would come closer and closer to shore.

There were times when we would all load up in the big Suburban and go on a "field trip" to the surplus store. Cheri's sister, Kim, and her son would go too. We would load up both vehicles full of dented canned food and other slightly damaged but safe and edible food stuffs. Loading up on non-perishable canned goods was important, because according to Cheri, the end of days was near. All we ever heard was how prepared we needed to be for Revelations in the New Testament Bible. To survive the end of times, we took this field trip every month. The shelves in the carport Dad had built were beginning to overflow with bulk food items.

About a year after we moved, Kim finally got divorced and bought a lot near ours and built a house. Then she spent a lot of time at our house, following in her sister's religious footsteps. She was over practically every day.

Kim's son was Ben. His name got changed to Paul. "This is the name God wants for you," Cheri said, excited to have a larger congregation of believers to lead. Cheri also changed Kim's name to Ruthie, which was from the Old Testament Bible.

Ruthie homeschooled her son, Paul. He protested at first. "It is God's will for us," Ruthie blurted out after a groan from Paul who shoved at the homeschool books that lay in his place at the table. Everything seemed to revolve around God speaking through our stepmom, Cheri.

Later, as I got older, I saw other people when we were out grocery shopping and wanted to be like them. I wanted to be normal like them, but I never told Dad and Cheri, because I would only get into trouble for wanting to be "worldly."

Any decision, even simply rearranging rooms in our home, would cause Cheri to pray to God. She moved furniture once a week, because she would pray about it, and God would want it moved elsewhere all the time. She would move the pictures around or the big rug in the living room.

"How silly," I thought to myself.

Twelve

Cheri's sister finally got the divorce
papers signed, and Ruthie cleaned her husband
of his money. He was a Texaco Oil guy. Cheri
talked him into giving her and her sister, Ruthie,
everything, which was what God wanted. But
really, it was for us, because Cheri took it all for
Dad and us kids. We all packed up and moved
to New Mexico to get away from the ex-
husband.

Cheri was the manipulator; she was using
the notion that God was speaking to her as a
way to convince her sister and Dad to do
whatever she wanted. Cheri told her sister's ex-
husband that he needed to get with God, and
then, maybe Ruthie would reconsider their
relationship. He had been a bit of a drinker and
had a temper that Cheri said was an ungodly
spirit when he drank. Demons were in him, and
he needed to get with God to be free.

Bobbie, Ruthie's now ex-husband,
responded with, "Ba humbug." He was
laughing it off as a big joke. When the divorce
was finalized, I felt sorry for him. I did not
think it was quite right for Cheri and Ruthie to
take him for all his money. Cheri said God
wanted us to move to New Mexico.

I always liked going on field trips, especially long ones. When Cheri announced God wanted us all to take a trip to New Mexico, I hollered, "Yeah, hip hip hooray!" I was so bored and tired of our religious lifestyle. Being a teen was extremely tough, and I thought a new place was what we all needed as a bigger family, a break from religion.

Our first trip to New Mexico was awesome; we bought a cheap Class C motorhome with Aunt Ruthie's divorce money. We explored the Ruidoso gold mining town and Rock hounding state park.

On the second trip we took, we spotted the land on the hillside of the campground where we would stay. It overlooked the Sierra Mountains. The beautiful tall ponderosa pine trees lined the entire expanse of the property. Dad, Cheri, and Ruthie (who was now like Cheri's religious twin) prayed about the land all day.

"God has a new sanctuary for us to continue to hear His Almighty voice here in New Mexico. We shall call it Joseph Land," Cheri exclaimed the next morning after the Bible study. Excited and overjoyed, I ran up and down what was soon be our land, breathing in the crisp fresh mountain air and taking in the gorgeous view that spread wide in front of the hillside mountain top.

Loading up the camper and large U-Haul trailer seemed to take forever. Our Texas home and Ruthie's new home sold easily. We parted with our swimming pool and landscaped yard. Out front, we also left a koi pond and wooden bridge Dad had built to go across the pond for decoration.

The drive to New Mexico was not very long. We were only a state away. The new high mountain altitude killed my grapefruit tree that I had planted back in spring from seed. The tree was almost as tall as me with poky thorns by the summers end. I was so proud of starting the seed from a delicious fruit I had plucked from a local Texas tree. It had sprouted up so fast, I felt like I had Mom's green thumb.

The New Mexico mountain air proved too tough on the thorny tree or anything else I later tried to grow. I felt just like the tree. I was withering inside, dying slowly from being so sheltered and secluded. I was away from society and had no friends my age to interact with in a productive, independent teenage way. I had no social skills at all.

I held my chin up in hopes that this new place would prove different from Texas. I prayed I would be allowed a new friend here, but my hopes were dashed quickly by Cheri announcing we would be living in the camper until the log cabins were built. This was what God wanted for us the next spring.

"Seriously," I mumbled under my breath. There was no way I wanted to live in that cramped camper with five brothers and sisters and Cheri and Dad. A small trailer was on the edge of the property, and that is where Ruthie and her son stayed.

Cheri bought this land in New Mexico, in the mountains near Alto, outside Ruidoso. She bought our motorhome, a Coachman, and we lived in it on the land. It was very crowded.

The new cramped lifestyle was almost unbearable. Beth, Rebekah, and I squeezed into the upper bed in the front of the Coachman. Two of the three boys slept on the table that folded down to a bed. The oldest slept on the floor. His legs stuck out into the hallway, and they would not fit on the small area the two younger boys shared. He had recently hit a growth spurt.

Dad and Cheri had a teensy bit of privacy in the rear of the camper. A make shift door closed off what held another table that converted down to a bed when pushed.

I had previously hated being sent to my room in Texas, but at least there, I had my own big bed in the shared girl's room. This was too much.

I am not sure how I lasted in those surroundings for almost a year, but I did. Each morning we took turns getting dressed in the only bathroom that was big enough to stand in. If I bent over too much, I would hit the sink, or if I leaned to far back, I would fall into the toilet. It was too small for one person, and our family totaled eight; it was horribly intolerable. I felt squeezed in, confined, and there was no escape in site. It was miserable for all of us.

Cheri and Dad had plans to build cabins that they had drawn up on blueprints. God had wanted us to build two cabins, one for the sister and one for Cheri and us. There were a lot of logs on the land, and we started to cut the trees down. Then we started to dig for the foundations.

My sisters and I helped haul the branches into a big pile after Dad and the boys cut the trees with a chainsaw. It was hard, back-breaking work, and each of us kids pitched in the best we could.

I enjoyed the cool mountain breezes and short thunderstorm bursts that seemed to pop up almost out of nowhere, providing a short break from tree clearing.

At this point, I was starting to get rebellious, very rebellious. I was eighteen and wanted to leave, but Dad wanted me to become a missionary. I did not want to be a missionary. I wanted to go to college. He said that that was man's knowledge, and I needed to find out what my spiritual gift was from God, so I could help other people. I said, "Okay," but I did not want to be a missionary.

I was scared, because I had never lived outside the house. I was so sheltered. I did not want to go overseas. I thought I had to live on my own a bit and get normalized. Dad was not happy with me wanting to move out and go to college. I had put my foot down, and that was what I was going to do, take it or leave it.

So Dad talked about it with Cheri, and they said they would at least help me get a job and move out. There was a Christian camp nearby. They said they would help me get this job, since it provided room and board. Imagine that. I did not have a social security number because Dad never got them for us. Even worse, at nineteen, I had no driver's license. I had to get a social security number and a picture id, because I did not have a driver's license.

I waited until I was nineteen to leave instead of eighteen so as not to hurt Dad's feelings. I had been Daddy's girl for so long, he saw me as a child and not an adult. I felt like an adult now and wanted to be treated accordingly.

During that last year, I rebelled a lot. I wanted to be normal. I could not go anywhere by myself. They told me that when I wanted to go on a bike ride by myself or go for a walk by myself that I could not. They thought they had convinced me that the Bible was the only way to live. One time, I got so fed up I took off and went up the mountain, but I came back, because I did not know anyone. I did not know how to get a hold of my older brothers and sisters. I did not have any food or water.

One time, Cheri put extra butter on my toast at breakfast, and she tried to do it sneakily, but I saw, and it was soggy and soppy and disgusting, so I threw the plate of food on the ground and walked out. And of course, I had a monkey on my back when I got back, and I had to be prayed over.

I could not handle it anymore. Almost every day, I was in trouble, having to apologize, having demons on my back. Sometime, they said they stayed up all night praying for me, and they blamed me for it, like it was my fault they had to pray for me. I was the oldest, and they said I needed to set a good example for the younger ones. I would say that I was doing the best I could. Deep down, I did not care for the way we were living anymore, I just wanted out.

Another time, we were coming back from shopping, and the cops pulled us over because we were not wearing seat belts. I wanted to stay home that day instead of going with everyone, but they reminded me that God wants everyone to go, so I went. When we got pulled over by the cop, Dad got a ticket.

On the way home, Cheri turned around and said it was my fault that we got pulled over, because I was in rebellion to God for wanting to stay home that day. Dad said that when we got on the road, that we could take our seat belts off. Wearing them was man's law, and God was our protector and healer, so we did not need to wear seat belts. So we took them off. I did not start wearing my seat belt until later, when I moved out and got fined three times. God's view on seatbelts was not going to work, obviously.

If anyone asked us how we were doing,

we were supposed to say we were fine, even if we were not. I did not think that was honest, so I asked why I was supposed to lie. Cheri said that people on the outside world would not understand our living-with-God lifestyle and would take it the wrong way. Living how God *wanted us to live* was not something everyone would understand, so it was okay to lie, letting people hear what they wanted to hear, not necessarily the truth.

When we went on outings, we were supposed to stay together, not cause any commotion. We were not to talk to anyone. Someone at a grocery store with their shopping cart came near us and said, "You have such a nice quiet family, such obedient, well-mannered kids." Cheri said, "Thanks, they sure are, aren't they?"

Deep down, I was very upset and felt like we were a cult. It did not feel right. I felt enslaved. I started to hate the way we were living, which is why I rebelled so much at the end. I started to see our life in a different light. I could not take being so controlled. It did not seem godly to me. It felt fraudulent.

Dad marrying Cheri and our families joining together was a huge mistake. We never had phone privileges, and even if we had had them, we had no friends to call. We were not allowed to have any contact with our older brothers and sisters, because they were not of God.

We were not allowed to wear red or eat strawberries or pineapple, because these things were of the Devil. Cats were bad, especially black ones.

When we got dressed, we had to show Cheri or Dad what clothes we were going to wear. We had to get permission to wear the clothes we chose. If I had a pair of jeans that were a little snug in the rear, I had to change into looser fitting ones. If a shirt was too flashy, I had to put on a plain one. When we went for car rides, we could not look at the people in the other cars. If I smiled at a cute boy in another car, Dad would give me an evil look.

A funny thing happened when we lived in Texas. We went on a road trip to Galveston. We went to the beach to watch dolphins. On the way there, we three girls were sitting in the back seat of the station wagon. We thought it would be fun to play a game. On the way to the beach, we would wave at everyone that drove by. We would mouth, "Hi," and see how many would wave and smile back. It was a simple game we made up to pass the time.

We did this to every single person that drove by. A few people we passed would honk their horns, wave, and smile. Dad and Cheri wondered what was going on. They finally looked back and realized what we were doing, and told us to stop.

We did stop trying to communicate with people on the road. But, we were looking forward to talking to strangers, if that is what it took to engage in a decent conversion. We rarely had a chance to, and it barely ever happened. They made us feel afraid to speak to anyone, anytime.

I could not take it anymore and was willing to take the chance and talk to any stranger, if that is what it took. I did talk to someone, and they strongly recommended I get out as soon as possible. I decided I was going to leave that evening.

I was fed up, and I ran away toward the mountains. The sun started to set low and the temperature dropped, sending shivers through my thin sweatshirt. I was getting hungry from the long trek up, so I hung my head and went back, thinking how much trouble I would be in.

I got back, and it was getting dark out. Dad and Cheri said I should not run away because there were bad people out there who could rape me and kill me and throw me in the woods, and no one would find me.

I had to read my Bible again for the umpteenth time and apologize for leaving. I did as I was told, but did not feel sorry for leaving one bit, and I expressed my desire to move out for real.

Thirteen

A Christian camp was nearby in Capitan, New Mexico. Dad and Cheri hoped this would slowly ease my need to adapt into society, the real world.

At the local Christian camp, there was an opening for a cook's assistant. Cheri and Dad asked me if I was sure I wanted to move out and take a job like this.

I think in Dad's eyes, I was still a kid, not nineteen. He pulled me aside and reminded me that living outside our household would not be easy. I would have to get identification. I would have to earn money, and I had to live alone. These three things scared me. It seemed overwhelming.

Dad cried when I left to go to camp. I had never seen him cry for anyone before, not even Mom. He reluctantly helped me load my belongings. I also took my hot pink ten speed bike. I got this with my paper route money. He took me to the camp.

I think he let me go because I was acting up every day, and I think he was sick of it. After I repeatedly refused their offer to send me off to do mission work, they felt like they had no other choice but to help me move out. I am sure saying goodbye to me was the hardest thing

Dad had done since the time Mom died. His crying greatly shocked and saddened me. I got a lump in my throat, and my heart was racing abnormally.

I actually felt a little guilty for not doing the mission work he so wanted me to do. I waited from age eighteen to nineteen, a whole year, for Dad and Cheri to see things my way. We were all stubborn though, and a truce was as good as things would get. It was time for me to leave, and I was through with waiting.

I did not think I would miss the way we lived. I got out of the car, gave him a hug and said goodbye. The goodbye was short and sudden. Dad's face was sad. It was as if he was looking right through me when he said goodbye and turned to go.

It was the beginning of my new life in the world, and it was the end of the secluded religious life I had known. It hit me all of a sudden, like a cold, hard slap to the face. I did not consider, at the time, that they were in the process of disowning me like they had my older siblings, but they were.

I worked at the camp. I helped the cook in the kitchen prepare and serve meals to the camp kids. It was busy during the day, but at night, I missed my family. I did not know why I was sad and missed my previous home. I wanted to be free, and now that I was free, I missed them all. At night, I cried myself to sleep.

I had my own camper to sleep in at the campground where I worked. At first I was excited because I was free and had all this space, but then that scared me. I did not know what I wanted to do. There was a whole world out there, and I did not even know how to live in it. I did not know how to eat, drive, or socialize. I was so controlled by Cheri's rules that I did not know how to think for myself. I got down to 95 pounds. I felt weak and miserable.

My first free weekend, I had laundry to do, but I decided to go home to visit and do my laundry there. When my ride pulled up to drop me off, Dad, Cheri and the kids got out of the camper and looked down at me from the hill up above. I started walking up towards the camper, and they told me not to come any closer.

I said, "What?"

Cheri crept down the hill, telling the others to stay back at the camper as if I had leprosy or something. I had only been gone a week or two. Cheri came down and said that I was not welcome on their property.

I asked why, and she said, "You made the decision to move out and live out in the world, and now you're no longer welcome to visit or be on the property anymore."

I shouted, "What do you mean, I was just here?"

She turned and walked away, saying nothing more. Cheri's sister, seeing me perplexed, came down the hill to my eye level and sternly said, "You look like a skeleton at death's door. God wants you to repent of your sins now!"

My hopes of maintaining any relationship upon leaving were abruptly dashed. I spun around and started crying softly to myself as I walked back to the car, all numb inside with my dirty laundry. I did my laundry in town.

I did not eat for a while, and I was down to 87 pounds. The camp counselor noticed this. Being concerned for my well-being, he took me to the doctor for my first physical ever. I did not have my period for quite some time because I was so underweight.

"Everything looks fine." The doctor patted my shoulder as I got up to leave; he was surprised I had never been to a doctor or had a physical before then.

I just shrugged my shoulders in response, not wondering why it was a big deal. Instead, thinking back, I realize how lucky I was that I never truly came down with anything serious. We always believed God was our healer and our doctor at home. I was confused at what to believe. I was not sure, but maybe God did gift doctors to help people on earth. There was a battle going on inside of me, and part of me wanted to believe in the version of the Bible that Dad and Cheri had raised me to believe. The other part of me was thinking that the world was not so completely evil, as I had been taught.

I was like my older brothers and sisters now, disowned for leaving *the religion*. So I wondered if I could get ahold of them, and I searched for a phone book when I got back to the campground.

I knew my oldest brother owned a bar in Cedar Rapids. I learned this from eavesdropping on a conversation Dad and Cheri had in the past. I could not find his number, so I called directory assistance. I got a number, called the bar, and asked for Jess Macho.

He spoke slowly, hesitating at first, not recognizing my voice. "Hello, who is this?" He said.

My heart was pounding wildly, and I was barely able to contain my composure after the recent laundry incident. "It's Blessing, your younger sister."

He did not say anything for a minute, which seemed like forever to me. I told him that I had just moved out, and he asked where I was. I explained that I moved to a religious camp, and that I was hurt, lonely and disowned. I told him I felt that nobody cared about me, and I did not know what to do, so I called him.

He was excited and overwhelmed, and said he wanted to tell the others. "I'll talk to them, and let's see what we can do to help you," he exclaimed, all giddy with excitement.

I questioned myself on why I had not gotten ahold of him or the other siblings sooner. There seemed to be nothing evil or witchy about them. They were the ones wanting to help me. I did not understand and was beginning to wonder if anything Cheri had ever said was really from God, or was it just her need for complete control? I was like a puppet, and she had been pulling my strings for a long time.

A week later, they had made arrangements to get me back to Iowa. I went to visit Conny in Texas first, since she was the closest. I went on a small plane. This was my first plane trip ever, and the thunderstorm that shook my seat scared me. I hugged tightly to my chair and said a prayer.

Upon arriving, Conny's face lit up and our embrace was heartfelt. The tears of joy, after being apart for so long, flowed freely down our faces. I never really had a chance to spend quality sister time with her. She moved out when I was still young.

I stayed with Conny and her husband for a couple of days. We went to AstroWorld, because I had never been to a theme park. I drank a lot of diet soda, because it had been off limits to me too. That was another one of Cheri's rules.

Tall roller coasters raced me around, making me dizzy, but I had so much fun, I could hardly contain myself. The rides were so fast and twisty. I had a blast. I loved going on the big coasters the most, and so did Conny's husband. I think we went on one ten times until Conny put her foot down, saying it was getting late, and she wanted to cook me a fancy turkey dinner, so we had to get going.

I was skinny and under-weight. I looked like a skeleton from being so depressed after leaving Dad and Cheri and them disowning me. Conny cooked a fabulous golden turkey. We sat down and pigged out. As we ate, I shared how sheltered my life had been.

Conny gave me an array of stylish, new clothes. I was overjoyed as I picked up a pair of white Gap jean shorts and held them up in front of me to see how they looked in the mirror. I was smiling from ear to ear.

My sister was elated to help me in any way she could, and she expressed her concern for my safety and well-being now that I was on my own. I assured her that I was fine, and that I was looking forward to seeing all of the other siblings back in Iowa.

She dropped me off at a Greyhound bus terminal a few days later. The fun days had flown by, and as I said my goodbyes, I reassured her I would visit and call often, now that I was on my own, free to make my own decisions. My brothers and sisters paid for my bus ticket.

As I sat down, I had some time to reflect on what had happened since I left the Bible camp. I never really seemed to fit in there, but everyone seemed to like me. It was a good experience, but it was time for me to be with family and have some kind of life. It was not really sinking in yet that I was totally free.

The Christian leader of the camp, and others at the camp, encouraged me to contact my older brothers and sisters. I was amazed by how pretty the camp leader's house was. I wondered why my family was so weird and different. This man was a preacher, and they were normal; why wasn't my family? It was confusing because I thought the way we were raised was the only way to live.

This led me to think that my parent's beliefs were not valid, even though it had been all I had ever known. I cannot believe now that I ever thought they were righteous.

At the camp, I did not feel like I was out in the real world yet, and I still did not have people my own age to hang out with. I was lonely and stand-offish, and they were worried for me, so they encouraged me to contact my siblings. I am mighty glad I did. This probably saved my life.

Fourteen

I skipped all the way to my seat on the enormous Greyhound bus. I was excited to see all the people and was thinking about how many new friends I could make on my way up to Iowa. I flew to Houston, Texas, then I jumped on a Greyhound bus to Cedar Rapids.

I was elated that there were a lot of people on the bus, and I was happy I could sit next to anyone. There was a guy all dressed in black. His nails were painted black, and he looked sad and depressed. I thought I could cheer him up so I sat by him. I started telling him a little bit about my life and wound up preaching the gospel. I thought it would be great sharing God's word with him. I commented that he seemed a little down, and I thought maybe I could cheer him up.

He said, "No, you can't, there's nothing that can cheer me up." Everything he said was negative. He hated everything.

I was anxious to make him feel good and put a smile on his face. It did not bother me that he was getting a little bothered and irritated by me. I did not know the bus driver had been eyeing us the whole time. He did not like the way this guy in black was behaving.

I thought I was doing a good job of

cheering him up. The bus driver pulled the bus over at a gas station and people thought it was a normal stop, but it was not.

As I was getting off, he pulled me aside and told me to wait until everyone had gotten off because he wanted to talk to me. He said, "You don't understand, you could have been in danger, and that guy was getting mad at you."

I said, "No, I didn't understand, I was just trying to be nice."

The bus driver suggested that I sit up front near him for a while. I was a little confused, but I agreed and took my new seat by him.

At another stop, a guy got on the bus that had just gotten out of jail. He had tattoos all over his body. He was a big, scary looking guy sitting all by himself. This guy also seemed sad or down, and I thought I could cheer him up.

He was sitting in the back alone, and I sat by him. I think I was overly talkative and overly exuberant. I wanted to be a friend with someone. I wanted to feel like I had a friend. I started telling him about my life and how I had been raised religiously. He did not look up at me, so I continued blurting out scripture versus. He did not want to be bothered, but I kept talking.

The bus driver stopped the bus again and firmly pulled me aside one last time. He requested I sit behind him again. He told me that I should not start talking to any stranger.

The stern look he gave me convinced me to heed his warning, and I obeyed this time.

I met a friendly girl on the bus, and we sat together. I decided maybe it was best I not talk religion to anyone else, unless they brought it up themselves. We talked about fruit trees.

The long hours flew by as we chatted away, and soon we were in St. Louis, Missouri. Jenny offered to let me stay the night with her. I said, "Yes, I'd like that because I have nowhere to wait for my next bus to take me to Iowa."

It was very late. I was pretty scared in the enormous, strange bus terminal.

A hot meal and cozy bed awaited us upon our arrival. I was comforted by the warm welcome her family gave me. We had a nice dinner and talked late into the evening. We were tired from our travels, so we turned in and got a great night sleep. I thanked them all repeatedly when they brought me to the bus station the next day. I thanked Jenny, got her name and number, and thanked her for her and her family's generosity.

Remembering the driver's warning from the day before, I sat with a girl again; she was less talkative and read her book most of the way. I happily peered out the window, thinking of the brothers and sisters I had missed for so long. When I saw cornfields, I knew we were close to Iowa.

I was elated and full of nervous emotions when the bus pulled up to the little terminal in

Cedar Rapids, Iowa. Anxiously waiting for me were all four siblings, eager to hug me as soon as I got off of the bus. I hardly recognized them; it had been so long since I had seen them.

"I hardly recognize you, you are so small and skinny," Lilly blurted out rather bluntly, as though she had read my thoughts. We formed a big group hug, and my brother, Gregg, grabbed my only luggage, which was my banana box. My hot pink ten speed bike would not fit on the small plane, so I had given it to one of the camp kids.

They all wanted me to spend time with each of them, so it was arranged that I would stay a little while at each of their homes. I could share my experiences about life with Dad and Cheri and my life in New Mexico. I could also share how hard it had been for me, there at the end. I could now start slowly transitioning into society.

That night, at Gregg's apartment, I had a dream and Cheri was in it. It was a flash back of her early years as my stepmother:

It was my first birthday after Mom died. Cheri was going to make a fancy cake; she knew Mom often did this. She made a plain cake; it was rectangular and still in the pan. My Mom always made cakes with layers, and they were pulled out of the cake pan and put on a fancy plate. She always added flowers and piping and put decorations on them. They were never just a plain cake. I pretended to think it was great so as not hurt Cheri's feelings. It was awful compared to what Mom would make, like eating cardboard.

Cheri was trying way too hard to win me over, and I was not going to have any part of it. I was not going to forgive her for burning all of Mom's things.

Later she did not try to win me over at all; she just tried to get me into trouble with Dad. She told Dad I was rebelling, and she blew things out of proportion to get Dad on her side.

I also had a dream the next night. It was another flash back, and this time, I was doing laundry. I put darks with lights and added some bleach. The color bled onto the lights, and the darks were a little bleached. Cheri said I did it on purpose, and I should go pray. These were my dreams back then.

I apologized to Gregg, one day, for watching a provocative show on TV, and he gave me a funny look and said, "What are you apologizing to me for? Don't you see you did nothing wrong?" I found myself constantly saying I was sorry for things when it was not needed.

I was struggling inside, trying to fight off the controlling ways that Cheri still seemed to have over me. I was having a hard time adapting into society. I was worried that I did not have any skills that would help me get a job.

Gregg told me I could babysit his one year old son, but that only lasted a week or so. I did not have the knack for it, anymore. I was scared and unsure about what I should do when he cried.

I lasted at Jess's home above his bar for only a few days. It was just too distracting, and the room I was to stay in was cramped. It was bursting at the seams with him and his girlfriend's belongings. She also liked her privacy and was not too keen on sharing it with Skinny-Minnie me.

I overheard her tell Jess that this was not an ideal situation. She said I was too malnourished and needed more help than they could give me. Jess reluctantly agreed, although he did let me stay another day. I was glad, because I was going to miss his two, big, fluffy dogs that I adored from the moment I saw them. I was sorry to go, but it was easy to see that his place just was not going to work out, and that was fine.

Fifteen

My weight was at an unhealthy eighty-three pounds. My siblings wanted to help me with this. They were all willing, but they were not sure what to do for me. They talked to my Aunt Wendee who seemed very concerned about my weight.

After meeting with Aunt Wendee and Uncle Jo, they agreed to let me stay with them. I was there for a week. I felt down, because I had trouble adjusting to the world and did not know why I was having difficulty getting a job. I wanted to hurry up and adjust. I did not really know how to eat right. I was used to having everything given to me. It became too much for me to handle, so they put me in the hospital. I gained some weight there, but it was not a place where I could feel at home. I felt like my problems were unlike anyone else's. I said I wanted to go back home to Dad.

Lynne came to me, a tear running down her cheek. She gave me a squeeze and offered to help me. She told me I looked a lot like Mom, now that I was grown up, and she asked me if I knew that she had seen Mom pass away at the hospital. I said no.

I had fallen back to sleep after they took Mom to the hospital. Lynne proceeded to tell me how Gregg had pelted her apartment window with rocks the night Mom died. Lynne frantically turned on her phone after Gregg told her about the incident. Dad had been trying to reach Lynne, but she had her phone turned off because Lilly usually called late to talk when she was drunk.

The phone immediately rang, now that the ringer was turned back on, and Dad's scared voice on the other end said Mom was at the hospital. If Lynne wanted to see her one last time, she had better come quickly. Lynne hastily woke her husband and joined Gregg, who was impatiently waiting in the car.

At the hospital, Lynne almost knocked some stranger over as she raced down the bleak corridor to where Mom was. There, she met Dad and the other siblings who sat quietly around Mom's bed. Lynne started crying as she held Mom's cold hand and said a simple goodbye.

Dad asked everyone to hold hands and say a prayer for Mom. Lynne agreed and felt a peace overtake Mom's room, almost as if Mom was telling everyone present goodbye.

Lynne hugged me close, and I hugged her back. Lynne said I could come live with her in her trailer. It was already tight with Lilly, Lynne, and Lynne's husband living there together.

I got my first job at Burger King, a few blocks away from where Lynne lived. I was glad to be able to walk to work. I was a hard worker and got a fifteen cent raise after a week, which was a big deal for me.

I worked there for about a year, and then I got a better job at McDonalds. They had some benefits, and there was more opportunity to get promoted.

I saved up to buy a car. Jess was going to teach me how to drive, since I never had had a driver's education classes.

Jess had his hands full, teaching me how to drive. Neither he nor any of my other siblings were evil like Cheri and Dad had said they were. They were wrong to have drilled this into our young minds. They just could not have been further from the truth; my siblings were going to be a great part of my life.

My sister, Lilly, was dating a guy that worked at a car dealership, and we thought my first car was within reach. I had about six hundred dollars saved up from my fast food jobs. Those few dollars bought me a baby blue Mercury Lynx.

I was so proud to be independent and own my very first car. I felt that I had come a long way that first year, even though I still missed Dad and my younger brothers and sisters. But, it was not every day and all the time anymore.

I had more bad dreams about Cheri getting mad at me for some simple mistakes that I made. I would wake up all sweaty, glad this was only a dream, and I really was not in trouble. I had to repeatedly remind myself that I was an adult now and could make my own decisions.

Whether right or wrong, things were for me to decide. My siblings had to keep reminding me that simple, everyday things were not bad things that I had to apologize for.

Dating:

Jess owned a bar and at night I would go and dance, and he and his bouncers all kept a close eye on me. At nineteen, I was going to Jess's bar to dance to pop music and drink diet sodas. I did this a few nights a week. I thought it would help me meet some people. I would see someone I thought was cute, but I would not know how to approach him.

Lynne and Lilly started to sit me down and tell me their experiences. They told me to find a guy that was not too pushy, was not a drunk, and was not one that just *wants in your pants*. You want a good guy that dresses nice, is well-mannered, he's approachable and wants to take you on a proper date, they told me. It was all kind of confusing and a lot to take in, but I listened and absorbed as much as I could, hoping for the best.

I had a couple of instances when I went to Jess's bar, and guys approached and asked me on a date. Jess was trying to be protective, as a big brother should.

There were a couple of guys that approached me that were told to stay away from me, I was off limits. However, Jess could not protect me from everyone all the time, and I ended up going out with a guy that Jess would not have approved of.

There was an instance when Jess was not keeping an eye on me, and this guy who was a bit of a drunk asked me to go to his place to watch a movie or two. I was not sure I should, but I was attracted to him and his blonde hair. I did not know what would happen, but thought I might as well break the ice some time.

I was almost twenty years old. We went to his place and we watched a movie. Then he started kissing me all over, and he wanted to go back to his bedroom. I told him the movie was not over, but he said it would be more fun in his room, and he kissed my neck and tried to unbutton my shirt. I did not hesitate at this point, because this was all new and interesting. He was kissing me more, so I kissed him back. He undressed himself, and I let him undress me. Things started happening so fast, and before I knew it, we were having sex.

I did not know it at that time, because I had never done it before, but I had heard it was supposed to be awesome and fulfilling for both people. But, for me, it was a letdown.

Everything happened so fast. It did not hurt, and I did not feel much of anything. I bled a little bit. When he was done, I said, "Did we just do it, is that it?"

He sleepily replied, "Yes."

He did not seem to care as he dozed off in a drunken stupor. I guess I was expecting more, at least a little foreplay or something, being that it was my first time ever having sex. I cleaned myself up and put my clothes on and hastily left. It was not very romantic, and I felt a little ashamed. I was embarrassed by how nonchalant he had responded, like I was nothing special to him, just another girl. This upset me, and I never called or saw him again. Now, I understood why Jess did not want *some men* around me. He was right; this guy was one of those bozos.

I wished Dad, Mom, or Cheri had explained the birds and the bees to me. I started to think that if what I experienced with that man was what a relationship really was, then it was not what I wanted. I decided to be more careful with myself around men. I felt dirty afterwards, like I should not have jumped into it with some stranger.

I went on more dates. There were a couple of short relationships, but the guys wanted to marry me right away and have children, but I did not feel ready, so I got away from them.

At this point, I started concentrating more on my job, and I got a decent promotion. I was still going dancing at night, and on one particular occasion, there were two attractive guys that came into the bar and watched me dancing. I thought they might be twins. I spotted them checking me out, so I strolled over and said hi, swaying my hair as I approached.

One said he was Rick, and the other said he was Pat, and it seemed like maybe they were a little shy. We had some small talk, but it only lasted a minute, and they seemed to disappear into the crowd. I guessed that was that and hoped maybe our paths would cross again. It did.

Sixteen

Rick came into McDonalds to get lunch. He had duct tape on his fingers. I asked him about the duct tape, and he said he did not have band aids, and his fingers would crack open in the winter from the dry air. He said he had just gotten back from Florida.

Rick was with a co-worker, and when that guy came up for a refill, I asked what Rick's last name was, and he told me. I asked if he had a girlfriend, and he said no. Then he asked, "Why, do you like him?"

I said, "Yeah."

He sat back down and must have told Rick, because Rick started looking at me, and we would glance at each other as I pretended to wipe tables clean.

They took a long time to eat their lunch. They got up to go, and I hesitantly asked Rick if he was married and he said no. I said, "A good looking guy like you not married and no girlfriend?"

He simply said, "Nope."

They left, and I could not stop thinking how tan he was, so I went to the tanning bed after work. I asked if I could use their telephone. I called every last name in the phone book that had his last name and I asked for Rick. When I got his Mom, she gave me his unlisted phone number.

I called him, and I said it was the girl from McDonalds, and I told him that his Mom had given me his number. I asked if he wanted to go out sometime, and he said sure. I asked him what he liked to do, and he said all kinds of things. He suggested a hockey game in the nearby Quad Cities that weekend.

We went to a hockey game that Friday, and that was our first date. He asked me what I wanted to do on our second date, and I said I liked movies. So, we went to an action movie. We had a great time. It seemed too good to be true. We went to a lot more movies, even when he was tired from pouring concrete all day.

After a movie, while we were holding hands, I asked him if we were boyfriend and girlfriend yet. He said, "Sure, why not."

I proceeded to tell Rick how we nearly did not meet because I had joined the marines, for a challenge, and to get college paid for with the G.I. Bill. I had done this a month before I met Rick.

I had pretty much given up on men and thought a change of life would be good for me, like a swift kick in the pants to motivate me again. I told my oldest brother Jess this, and he did not seem to understand, telling me he did not think it was a smart idea.

The recruiter I talked to made empty

promises to get me to enlist. They bragged of the awesome experience and great physical challenge. They promised me a job in the medical field. They then slapped me with a job washing dishes.

I could tell I had made a mistake joining the Marines, but there were only two ways to get out. One way was that I could be deemed mentally unstable. The other was to lose or gain too much weight. I immediately started dropping weight and lost ten pounds in one week, eating only lettuce and apples. I drank lots of water to deter the hunger pains that came from not eating.

They told me I had an eating disorder and was sent to the sick ward to await my departure and go home. I was released as though I had never enlisted. I was only there a few weeks and that was not enough to be considered active military. They said I could come back once my weight reached an acceptable standard.

Are you kidding, I thought to myself. I did not even look back as the plane took off. What a waste of my time, I pondered. Thankfully, I was out. I felt I had already had enough of a challenge with my stepmom's mind controlling, religious ways. I did not need the military's drill sergeant criticizing me too.

What I liked about Rick was his good looks, those baby blue eyes and blonde hair that curled slightly on the end. I also found out he was a hard worker. I liked the hard working mentality in him from the beginning.

We moved in together after a year. We bought a duplex together which already had one tenant. We had to fix up one side because it sat empty for a while and had some plumbing issues, amongst other things.

About a year after we were together, Rick asked me if I wanted to go learn how to drive a semi. I said, "Sure," glad to get out of fast food work.

So, we went to a truck driving program at our local community college. We were going to graduate with a class A CDL and be team truck drivers. It was a six week course that held national honors for the top truck driving colleges. When we completed the course, we had a job waiting for us with a local company. We made good money and drove to all 48 states in two years. It was something Rick always wanted to do, and I enjoyed it too. It was awesome to see the whole country.

Before this point, I had hid my eating disorder from him, and everyone else for that matter. Once we were trucking, I could not hide it from him. I could not throw up anymore because there was no bathroom in our truck. When we would stop to eat, I could go throw up in a truck stop restroom. It was during these times that I thought about weaning myself away from bulimia. That is when he confronted me about it.

He knew the whole time that I had an

eating disorder, but I did not know that he knew. I told him I wanted to get better, and I started to eat good meals. I was not feeling guilty about eating healthy foods. I limited myself to purging on the weekends. After a while, I did not feel the urge to do it anymore, so I finally stopped.

Rick helped me see the disorder for what it truly was. I had been seriously consumed by bulimia over several years. It was not easy to do, because I liked food too much.

During our first year together, I told Rick a little about my upbringing. He suggested that if I missed my family so much, I should go visit them. He felt this would give me closure. He told me he would come with me if I wanted to go visit Dad, for moral support. He was concerned after I told him how the first visit went and was worried about me going by myself this time.

The first time I went back to New Mexico, I drove there in my car. It had been over a year since I had left. I had saved enough money to take my first vacation, and I was excited to go back to my old home in the mountains. It was around Thanksgiving time.

I showed up unannounced. I was afraid that if I told them I was coming, they might go out of town on purpose. Cheri had done that before to her own mother.

They were shocked when I arrived, and they did invite me in. Cheri said it would have been nice if I had called to let them know I was coming. They said that I needed to repent of my sins, that I needed to not be so worldly, and I needed to get back with God. They suggested I move back in with them.

I yelled at them and asked why we could not have a normal family visit. I also asked why they had to preach all the time. Cheri shouted, "Do you want us to be someone we're not? If God has something to say, then we say it."

Dad did not have much to say, though. They made the kids stay in the house. So, I left. I was upset and frustrated, mad that nothing had changed since I lived there. Cheri was even more controlling.

I attempted other visits, hoping that maybe Dad would change and not be so religious. This never happened. The only changes that occurred were that some of my younger siblings surprisingly left after they too were sick of being so sheltered and got fed up with all the religion.

When I went back to Iowa, I wrote some letters to Dad and Cheri. The first response I received from them was nothing but mumbo jumbo preaching. I thought I would fight fire with fire. I wrote back to them making references to the *prodigal son*, and I also quoted scripture that referred to not being judged. They responded back, but it was only to say that they were on a sabbatical and that they could not be bothered at this time. It was a while before I made any attempt to contact them.

I always wanted Dad's approval when Rick and I got engaged. So in 1999, Rick and I jumped in our motor home and headed for New Mexico for a surprise visit.

Again, I did not let them know we were coming. I do not know why Dad's approval was so important to me; maybe it was because he never approved of anything I ever did. It would mean a lot to me. I wanted to see Dad, and Rick was curious about the religion. He could not believe it was as bad as I said it was. He would soon see that I was not exaggerating.

No one was there when we arrived, but they soon got home. I introduced Rick to Cheri, and she liked him right away. She said Rick seemed humble and that might be good for me. He was experiencing a tooth ache and retreated back to the camper.

Dad did not have much to say, but he sure gave Rick a stern look when they showed up in their car. I was amazed that they let me in their house. Cheri immediately spouted that God's world was coming to an end. She said we needed to prepare ourselves for the end of days.

It seemed to be a better visit overall than the last time I had been there. Rick suggested that I bite my tongue if I needed to, that yelling at Cheri would get me nowhere. I needed to stay calm and act like I cared about what Cheri preached, even if I did not. Rick was proven right.

Our conversation went better than I ever expected, but it did not seem very heart felt. We stayed in the camper on their property that night. We got preaching for breakfast the next morning and decided between that and Rick's toothache, we should plan on heading home. I was glad we had a decent visit. It was short but turned out to be better than expected.

I guess I got all the approval I was going to get from the trip. When we decided we were going to get married, we invited them to our simple ceremony in nearby Las Vegas. They were not able to make it; they were busy doing God's work. I had wanted Dad to give me away, but I accepted that it was not going to happen.

My brother Jon came to the wedding and filled in for my Dad. He was on the verge of leaving Cheri and Dad. He needed to get away from them too. I told him that when he was ready, we were here for him, and we would help him get out on his own.

Jess, our oldest brother, had a construction company. I suggested Jess offer Jon an opportunity to become a part of his business. That would give my oldest and youngest brothers a chance to reunite. This idea ended up a success story. They are now partners in business and quite brotherly.

I stopped attempting yearly visits to Dad's. I was fed up with the preaching and Cheri's degrading speeches. I asked Jon how he could stand it, and he said that they did not preach to him like they did to me. His secret was keeping a low profile and not talking back.

I guess the reason I was treated like a sinner was because I would always talk back, and I would always speak up for what I believed in. I was never the perfect Christian they wanted me to be. That was okay with me. In my eyes, I was a good Christian.

Quite some time passed by before I went to see Dad and Cheri again. My next visit proved to be more peculiar than any before it. They wanted to stick magnets on me because they thought I was injected with a microchip when I went into the military. They thought the government could track people this way. They thought the magnets would distort the signal, and the government would not be able to pin point my exact location.

They wanted to be off the radar and not have any authorities know they existed. They also believed the metal fillings in my teeth or the soda that I drank from the store would boost the government's ability to track me. Cheri showed me various web sites trying to back up her claims. It was strange, and I said I would consider wearing the magnets.

I needed a break and decided to go to a nearby gym to relieve some stress. I was not going to wear magnets at the gym because people would look at me like I was a fool.

They wore magnets on their wrists and

ankles. I said I did not need the magnets because I would not be there much longer. They preached about the end of days again and how we all needed to be in hiding because the government was going to pick us off one by one. It would be like the genocide of the Jews. We were going to be a communist country and had to be careful.

I went to town, and on the way, I broke out crying and prayed that Dad could one day be normal again, even if it was just a little bit. I sat in my rental car and cried as I watched other families enter and exit the grocery store. I wondered why my childhood was so abnormal and distorted, why I could not have been like everybody else. What happened? All I wanted was a piece of true family life.

Rick did not go with me after the second visit because he did not like Cheri. He also worried they might brainwash me, and he would lose me to them for good. He told me Cheri was off of her rocker, and I should come home. The magnet thing was rubbing Rick the wrong way, and he almost wanted to come get me.

I simply replied, "No, I will be okay, I'm coming home tomorrow anyway. Don't worry, they brainwashed me too much before; it won't happen ever again!"

I brushed my tears aside and packed my bags at the hotel so I could get an early start in the morning. I had my own real home with Rick and our two newborn Chihuahuas: Tequila and Margarita.

Seventeen

Arriving back home in Iowa, I received an email from Cheri and Dad's website asking for $300 to help with missionary work in following God's will. I called the stepbrother who was still living with them and asked if they were really going on a mission trip.

"Of course not, they're just going to go gamble," he smirked, surprised that I did not already know. They would go gambling with the money people sent them to do God's work.

Cheri said God told her they were going to win big. Cheri, her sister Ruthie, Dad and Rebekah went once or twice a week, sometimes more if they were winning.

Rebekah was good at keno. This was a game I had never heard of, much less played, until later when she took me to a casino on one of my visits. Their missionary trips did not seem Godly to me. Cheri was scamming people and gambling with the money they sent to her. I was shocked and quickly deleted the email. I did not talk to them again for a year.

The next visit, I went with Gregg and Lilly. Dad had slipped and fallen and was not healing. He was moving slow and looked swollen, like a marshmallow. Gregg and I were very concerned. We told Dad he needed to get to a doctor, and we made that clear to the stepmom.

Lilly said something about how Rebekah looked good, and Rebekah said, "Thanks, it's because we have the same eyes, Mom and me."

We knew that Rebekah had been led to believe that Cheri was her real mother, though she was not. Cheri changed the subject and glared at us.

At some point, Cheri told Rebekah the truth, because at the next visit, I asked her if she knew that Cheri was not her real mother. She said she did know.

All those years, she had not known the truth about her own mother. I was disheartened and shaken up by this, but I still wanted to keep coming to visit Dad.

Our visit did not last long. Dad seemed tired and weak as I proceeded to tell him we were there to help him get better any way we could. He simply said okay, rather slow and quiet. Cheri barged in between us saying it was late and Dad needed his rest as she shuffled him off to the bedroom.

We found a free clinic for Dad the next day, and they took him. They found his teeth were infected and all needed to be pulled. He needed dentures, and we did not want to leave until something was done. He did get help. Cheri took Dad to Mexico, saying it was Gods will. There he got his teeth pulled and was fitted for dentures.

I visited again the following year. It was September, 2010. Gregg and I went to see how Dad was doing. He was still healing too slowly. We usually came unannounced. This time my stepbrother, Adam (who was a paramedic in Albuquerque), called late one evening and told me that if anyone else in the family cared about Dad, now was the time to see him.

Adam had done an exam on Dad, as best he could while visiting Cheri a few weeks earlier. Dad seemed to be having some trouble with his heart. He said something about fluid in his lungs and early signs of emphysema. I called all of the immediate family and franticly told them what Adam had said.

Most of the brothers and sisters could not leave to see dad quickly, because they had kids and work. Only Gregg and I went. The others asked me to evaluate the situation, and if I thought he looked too bad, then they might come. I had already seen Dad really bad, so I did not know how much worse he could get in a year's time.

I was anxious and nervous during the day-long drive to pick up Gregg. I hoped for the best and said a silent prayer. I hoped everything would be okay.

I was not ready for Dad to go yet, and deep down, I wanted him to live a lot longer. In fact, I could picture myself living close by if he was bedridden, helping care for his daily needs. I had already told Rick that I would do that if he got much worse. I was trying to prepare myself as best I could, and Gregg sensed my uneasiness and told me not to worry so much. He said everything would turn out okay.

When we showed up, the sun was slowly setting on the mountain side. A beautiful array of colors glowed across the dimming sky. The drive took a whole day, and we wanted to arrive before Dad's early bed time of seven pm. We barely made it. The hotel check-in would have to wait because we were on a mission to make sure Dad was okay, and nothing was going to stop us.

Upon our arrival, we were astonished to find Dad gingerly pedaling away on a stationary bike. Cheri knew why we were there and got right to the point, telling us how Dad was recouping nicely and most of the swelling had gone down from his face and body. In fact, he was due back in to get his dentures resized. The ones he had were too big, now that the swelling had subsided. Cheri also said he had been eating more fruits and vegetables and cut back on his smoking to one a day.

There was not much more I could have done to encourage his healing process. He was already doing everything I would have told him to do: rest, exercise, eat more fruits and vegetables, and stop or at least cut way back on smoking cigarettes. These were all things he was already doing, and I could not have been any more pleased with his progress. Dad did look remarkably better than a year ago. I nodded my approval to Cheri who seemed pleased with my relaxed demeanor.

Cheri had said when Dad and her first met, that it was okay to smoke in God's eyes. When God wanted Dad and her to quit, then they would. Obviously, that never happened, and Dad smoked like a chimney the whole time. I was amazed at everything Cheri told me. She proceeded to tell us how Dad was exercising on the bike every day for an hour, some times more, depending on how he felt. He was also taking herbal tea and vitamin c and other good vitamins too.

I almost could not believe my eyes when I saw how healthy Dad looked. I was so elated to see color back in his face. He was not puffy like a marshmallow anymore. He smiled as he pedaled away on his bike. Now, I just needed to hear him speak verbally and see how he responded. I was ready to put him in the hospital if needed.

I came over to the bike and bent down close to him. I finally told him the most important words in the world to me: "I love you. Do you still love me too?"

He stopped pedaling, looking me straight in the eyes. He said the words I so desperately needed to hear, "You know I do." He looked at me sternly but with such tender emotion.

Those were the last words he ever spoke to me. They were a little slow and slurred, but they were just what I yearned to hear. I broke down, melting inside. Tears flowed like a river down my face, and I hugged him with all of my heart. I needed to hear those three little words for some time and wanted to bottle up that moment for eternity. Gregg also came over and hugged him too.

It was hard for him to speak, so he did not talk that much. Dad did not look great, but he did not look like he was on death's door, either. Deep down, I knew Dad would want to die at home, not in a cold hospital. That was the way Dad was, and if he felt God calling him, it was his free will to live or die. Sadly, I realized the end was probably near.

Cheri invited us to dinner, but it was late, and we still had to get checked in to a motel. We said our goodbyes and headed down the mountain side. There was a feeling of peace as we left.

Dad died 10 days later. He was seventy-two years old. I got a phone call from Beth that he had died in the night.

Ironically, the heart rate watch on my wrist was beeping at the very moment that he passed. It was late, and all of a sudden, the alarm started beeping, even though I had not set it.

I pushed all the buttons, and it would not stop. Rick was sleeping soundly beside me, so I set it out in the garage hoping it would stop on its own. The watch would not stop beeping, and

I could not get back to sleep, so I thumped it a couple times to no avail. I was frustrated because it would not stop. I did not want to break it, since it always worked so perfectly. It was not cheap either, but I had no other choice. I took a hammer from the shelf nearby and smashed it into pieces. It stopped. It was not two minutes later when Beth telephoned me with the disheartening news that Dad had died.

Rebekah told me that Dad had woke up calling, "Help me, help me," as he gasped and gagged for air.

Cheri called 911. An ambulance came and checked his vitals and everything seemed to check out fine. However, as they got ready to leave, he stopped breathing rather abruptly. They paddled him, trying repeatedly to jump start his heart back to life, but he was so weak, nothing seemed to work. They pulled the sheet over him a short time later.

Rebekah could barely see the EMT working on him in the bedroom, but when they shook their heads at her, she cried and ran to her room, holding her dog tightly for comfort.

Eighteen

We found out, after the autopsy, that Dad had died of pneumonia. Cheri thought the denture cream might have poisoned him with too much zinc. It was standard procedure to have an autopsy performed when poisoning was suspected. They had to cut away some of his head in the procedure, so when I came for the funeral, to my dismay, I was not allowed to see him. The funeral director said it would not have been proper to view him in that state. I really wanted to see him lying there in the coffin, possibly so that reality could set in, and I would know he was no longer alive.

It was a shock to think Dad was dead. I had just seen him alive and healing ten days earlier.

I knew Dad was ready to go to the Lord and be with Mom again. Jess reassured me, after he saw me crying, that I should be happy for that, happy that neither Mom or Dad had suffered great pain or withered away in a nursing home.

It is a terrible thing to think that both Mom and Dad's deaths could have been prevented. Dad took Mom's anti-seizure medication from her and said God would heal her, but that did not work. The last seizure had proven lethal.

Dad's death was pneumonia, which could have been treated if discovered on time. Of course, Dad also had early signs of right side heart failure. He was in the early stages of emphysema from all the cigarette smoking, but initially, the autopsy results stated that the ultimate cause of death was pneumonia. There was no zinc poisoning like Cheri first believed. Simple antibiotics could have prolonged Dad's life.

I believe Dad thought it was God speaking to him. In a letter he had written to Cheri, he told her it was time for his weak, physical body to die, but not his spiritual one. He had quietly written the letter the day before he died.

When I showed up with my sibling, Cheri pulled the letter out and showed it to us. Tears ran down her cheeks. I had never seen Cheri act like that, and I think it was a struggle for her, not wanting Dad to go yet. I felt the same struggle.

I was emotionally a wreck inside, having cried my eyes out for days already. Rick comforted me as best he could before I left. I was trying to get ahold of my emotions, remembering the Bible verse that Dad read to us at a morning Bible study. It said there is a time and place for everything, even death. Rick reminded me that at least I got to visit Dad and tell him I loved him. I nodded as tears came to my eyes, remembering Dad. I squeezed him back, smiling, and said, "I'll be okay. I know deep down he's in a better place and at peace."

Jess pulled up and I hopped into his Escalade for the long ride to the funeral, and on that ride, I missed my Mom too. I kept the good, warm memories of her close in my heart, and now, I was going to have to do the same with Dad.

That was the hardest thing I had ever had to deal with besides Mom's passing. I was not prepared. It was hard to be prepared for a parent's death. I was heart-broken. Even though Dad and I had not been close at the time of his death, we had a lot of amazing memories and special times as I was growing up.

I wanted to ask him, during that last visit, about my mom. I wanted him to tell me, in person, that he did not want to hurt Mom by denying her the medicine she needed. I never did ask him. I felt that he was too weak, and I did not have the heart.

Most of us went to the funeral. Lynne and Lilly could not get off work. Jon, Jess and I all rode together. On the drive down, we reminisced about our childhood. Conny and Gregg had driven over the previous day.

Jon mentioned, the week before, how Dad wanted to be buried in a simple, wooden, pine box. It would be made from the ponderosa pines that grew on the mountainside there at the cabins. Adam and Beth were already constructing the large wooden pieces together when I arrived with Jess and Jon.

We had never built a coffin before, so we asked the funeral director for the measurements for one that was already at his office. He gave us the size so that it would fit in the hearse. On the way up to the cabins, we stopped at the local hardware store for supplies to finish construction. Each of us kids helped build and complete the coffin. It turned out to be large and unique, but simple in design. It was exactly what Dad had suggested to Jon at a previous visit a year or so prior.

The box was deep and large inside and out. The inside was lined with padding and crushed velvet, while the outside had heavy rope handles and a huge pine lid with an enormous carved wooden cross. Rebekah carved the cross. We stained the outside with a strong dark stain that brought out the wood grain colors.

We all worked together in harmony, creating the unique, massive structure. The peace and tranquility quickly ended as Cheri and I got into a heated argument. It got so loud and out of control that Jess had to step in to break it up.

I confronted Cheri because she wanted to blame us kids for his death, saying it was our fault he died, since we were not right with God and had not come to visit and see him more regularly.

I shouted, "How dare you put your religion into this; there is no one to blame for what happened."

Making us feel guilty was not appropriate, and I was not going to let her blame me or anyone else for anything, anymore. I was sick of it, and putting my foot down was empowering. I was fed up and offended to the core.

Rebekah got up crying, rushing off to her room with her dog Juno. Jess got in the middle of us, told us to calm down, and said this is not the time or place for this discussion. He stated that Dad would not have wanted us to be fighting. I stepped back, tears rushing down my face, and went outside to cool down. Cheri was strong willed, but I was too, now that I had grown up a bit.

We all helped make the pine coffin because that was Dad's wish. Now that it was finished, it took all the boys to heft it up into the back of the Escalade. Its next stop would be the funeral home, where Dad was resting on ice.

I did not like to think of him resting there, cold like that. I was told by the funeral director it was for preservation; having been gone almost a week now, he needed to be placed in the ground soon.

I felt deprived that I could not see him; I needed the closure. I told this to Jess and Jon on the way to the funeral. Jess said I should remember how Dad looked in good times, not how he looked in his pine box. "You don't want to have nightmares about seeing him dead, do you?"

"No, I sure don't," I answered.

We each had a hand in building the coffin and now that it was finished, a warm peacefulness overtook us. I felt proud to have taken part in Dad's final wish.

Once at the funeral parlor, the coroner was astonished at how unique and well-built the casket was. It barely fit in the hearse. He told us we did a great job constructing it and was surprised at how quickly we got it finished.

I knew if Dad could see, he would have been pleased with all of us kids pitching in and the special workmanship with the huge wooden cross on top.

The funeral director asked us how we were going to pay for the whole thing. Dad had no money to his name except a small social security check that barely paid for essentials as it was. Neither Dad nor Cheri worked, always telling me that God would provide. We decided to split up the expense between us kids. The military provided his resting place and a head stone. They also memorialized him with a twenty-one gun salute and flag ceremony.

Dad always kept the military-part of his life a secret. I think the military told Dad, upon his discharge, he was not allowed to divulge any information about his time in the Navy. I asked on many occasions and would pick up his white sailor hat twirling it on the tip of my fingers. I was curious to know of his exciting adventures in the Navy, but his answer was always short and sweet: "That was a long time ago, and little girls should not concern themselves with that."

I still wondered and would imagine my Dad on some big ship out at sea. One time, I inquired and he told me he worked with the radio as an engineer and never had to go fight on the front lines with guns blazing. He also told me he got to ride in a blimp once. "Cool!" I said. My eyes lit up at the thought of his excursions to faraway places so long ago.

After we paid for the service, the funeral director spoke about some of what Dad had done in the military, which up until then, I knew almost nothing about. He proceeded to tell us that Dad had received a medal of honor for time served. He helped create a flight simulator for what later became the stealth fighter jet.

I was shocked and amazed at Dad's engineering skills and capabilities. I flashed back, recalling the soybean grinder Dad made Mom out of an old ten speed bike that ground the soybeans into a fine powdered flour when ridden on. He also made a go-kart for the boys from a worn lawnmower deck and coffee cans.

Dad was like an engineering genius and could have gone far at his job at Rockwell Collins. However, he got saved by Jesus and quit his desirable engineering job there to follow the Lord, literally. I thought many times about how our lives would have changed, drastically, if Dad had not taken the Bible so fanatically.

Tears started flowing again down my face. Jess leaned over and hugged me, and I just let it go. I was emotionally drained, and that trip was taking its toll on me.

Dad was laid to rest at Fort Stanton, New Mexico, a mariner's military cemetery (because he served four years in the Navy). It was in between two mountain valleys, not far from their cabins in Ruidoso. He received a twenty-one gun salute ceremony for his time served. They also made a special head stone for him. They gave him a flag carefully folded for excellence in service and medal of good honor.

It was a bright sunny day that afternoon, birds chirping from a nearby tree. We all brought some flowers and cards from the local store in town. I brought a peace lily in hopes of it living on and not dying. I asked Cheri if she would plant it and water it from time to time when she visited Dad's grave. She said she would.

Rebekah played a song on her harmonica for Dad. It was a beautiful tune that filled the air. She had a hard time finishing the song as thoughts of Dad crept into her head from good times past.

When Rebekah finished, I stood up with a letter I had written the previous night. The letter was to my dad. It basically said that all of us children were here for him now. If he was looking down on us from up above, then here we were, back together as one united family. We now stood before him, better late than never. I finished my simple speech. There was silence. I wiped the tears from my cheeks and sat back down beside Conny.

After the funeral, we all loaded up and went back to the cabins to visit a bit with Cheri, her sister and Rebekah. I brought a picture album of our real Mom and was intent on showing it to Rebekah. I had to get Cheri's permission first. She reluctantly obliged but told me I had only an hour to do so. I was about to show Rebekah the first pictures of our Mom that she had ever seen. Cheri looked on from the room next to us.

Jon gave me a warning look as I walked past him to Rebekah. He did not want to see Cheri and I get into another fight. "I know," I assured him as I passed by to where Rebekah was sitting patiently, waiting with her dog Juno in her lap.

In the album was a clipping of Mom's obituary. This was proof for Rebekah that she had a birth Mom that had died when she was very young. She looked in awe at the album, seeing her name as a child of Mom's in the type print. There was a picture of her standing next to Mom in pink, heart-shaped sunglasses. She was smiling wide, Mom's arm wrapped snuggly around her shoulder.

I pulled the picture out and asked if she wanted it. "Sure," Rebekah replied, stating that she did not have any memories of Mom.

I could see from the glare in Cheri's eyes that she did not want me to overstep the chat I was having with Rebekah. As quickly as I handed her the pictures, I changed the subject.

She seemed to be happy in her situation, helping Cheri and her sister on a daily basis. She was an adult, and I did not want to rock the boat, but I told her as our hour was about up, that when, and if, she wanted to move out, Jon and I and the rest of her siblings would help her.

Rebekah knew she would be in trouble for visiting with me, so she went to her room, thinking how to please Cheri after we all left. She told me what happened at a later visit.

Sharing pictures of Mom and talking intimately to Rebekah lifted a weight off of my chest. We said our goodbyes. Jon, Jess and I packed up our small bags from the hotel and headed home. I made sure to let Rebekah know I would be checking in on her, after a while.

On the way home, I reflected back on Mom and Dad. It was a strange sensation, having someone I cared so much for die. I wished Dad had mellowed out a little before he passed. I had had high expectations that his fanatical religion would have relaxed a bit by that point. All I had wanted was happy get-togethers, quality family time. I missed the holiday fun we had when I was young, before the religion got out of control.

I missed the fun Thanksgiving dinners when the food was abundant, and relatives were laughing and chatting about happy things while Jon, Rebekah and I ran around playing with the cousins. I never ran out of hope, and I spent numerous times praying that one day, before Dad passed, things could be that way again.

I had a peacefulness overtake me on the drive back, a sort of vision, and it was Dad telling me that everything was fine. I should be happy for him now, not sad, like I was during the funeral. I smiled after this vision and told my two brothers about it. They seemed to also be in thought. It was almost like peacefulness came over all of us at the same moment that we were reflecting back about Dad and our childhood.

I miss my Dad, but mostly I miss the young years, when he was more like a Dad. I feel like I am still a Christian, even though I have been living out in society. I have not been fanatical or radical, more like a simple type of faith and belief in God.

I wondered how Rebekah was doing. She was the last one still living with Cheri. All the other siblings moved out, one by one, after I was gone. I hoped she had not gotten into trouble because I had shown and given her the pictures of our Mom. I was soon to find out.

Within a year's time, my phone rang one night. It was a call from my sister, Beth, telling me excitedly that Rebekah had moved out and wanted to talk to me.

I was so overwhelmed with emotion that I asked Beth for her number, so I could call Rebekah right that very instant. It was late, but I could not contain myself. I was shaking so much that I could barely hold the phone.

Nineteen

When I called her, she quickly picked-up. "Hello, how are you," Rebekah blurted out.

There was excitement in her voice as she spoke. I could tell Cheri was not standing over her to make sure she was not saying too much. We talked for hours. We were both in tears of joy, for it had been such a long wait. I thought the youngest sibling was finally out. What a huge relief.

She told me about how she met a cute Mexican guy who had helped her escape in the middle of the night by sneaking her out of the camper window while Cheri and Ruthie slept. Cheri had told Rebekah that it was not God's will for her to be dating. Rebekah had shouted, "That's it!" Later that night, her Mexican friend helped her escape.

Prior to her leaving, she, Cheri and Ruthie had loaded up the camper and headed to Mexico to get Rebekah's tooth fixed, and afterwards, they stayed in a tiny town called Paloma, to help a church with some missionary work.

Rebekah told me that she went up to Albuquerque to meet Jon. Jon brought food and supplies for the mission, and he warned

Rebekah to be careful, being across the border and all. Jon also reminded her that we would help her when she was ready to move out. The timing must have been right, because not long after he offered, Rebekah called him. When I talked to her, I gave her Gregg and Conny's number.

Rebekah told me, during that long phone call we had, that when she snuck out in the middle of the night, she left a note for Cheri on the camper's table in the kitchen. It stated that she was going to live with stepbrother Adam in Albuquerque, so Cheri did not need to be worried that she might have been abducted.

Rebekah also talked to a Mexican friend the next day who informed Rebekah that Cheri seemed to be acting normal, like nothing was wrong since Rebekah left. Rebekah said she felt better knowing that, and she did not want to have any contact with Cheri, now that she was out. It was too soon, and she did not feel strong enough to face her stepmother yet.

She did feel concerned for Cheri and her sister in that hot camper. The searing, summer heat with no working A/C was almost unbearable. Her dog Juno was getting old too. She was hoping they would move into the church facility house that they had been living next to while doing the missionary work.

At first, Cheri and her sister stayed in the camper at the border town of Deming and made trips some thirty miles south to Paloma, Mexico.

With passports obtained, Cheri decided God wanted them to move down to Paloma to be closer to the church they were helping.

Rebekah was not sure this was a good idea because of the violence in nearby towns. Cheri proclaimed, "God is our protector, and with the church on our side, there is nothing to worry about; just have faith in God."

Rebekah told me the local water was okay for a while, but when the summer heat started kicking into gear, the water became smelly with a pungent iodine taste. The town then offered free purified water behind a gated area in the morning from 8-9a.m. and also at noon. They started drinking the free water then.

The church house facility had a shower room that Cheri, her sister and Rebekah used, because their old camper had some plumbing issues. Rebekah missed her spacious room at the cabins in New Mexico and the freedom to carve her honey bears and sell them on her own.

Cheri had once warned her of becoming too worldly and independent with her bear money, saying it was a sin. Rebekah tried not to make too much and always gave Cheri and her sister the earnings she made. She put the money in an account Cheri had set up for all of them to share. Rebekah never used any of the money for herself. She was afraid of getting into trouble, so she only used her money to pay bills or get food for all of them.

Rebekah then told me that something had

happened to set her off. Ruthie and Cheri had been drinking all day at a country bar store, and Rebekah offered to drive home. Cheri said no, she was going to drive. Ruthie had a guy hanging all over her, drunk, kissing her, and he proceeded to tell them to come to his house to party. Cheri was drunk too and got behind the wheel, not listening to Rebekah's pleading for her not to drive.

On the way to the party, Rebekah was upset with them and jumped out while Cheri was driving. Rebekah walked the rest of the way home, hurting inside because they would not listen to her.

The next day when Cheri pulled up to the camper with her sister, Rebekah saw a bloody gash on Cheri's head. Cheri glared at Rebekah and said it was her fault for jumping out and leaving them. Cheri had lost control of the jeep, hitting a rock. She fell out of the jeep and had hit her head. Cheri said Rebekah was disobeying God by not partaking in the partying and drinking, reminding her that God always wanted the three of them to be together in activities at all times.

When Rebekah told me this, it brought back the memory of the ticket that Dad had gotten from the state trooper because none of us were wearing seatbelts. Cheri had said that it was my fault the cop pulled us over, because I wanted to stay home and not go as a group to the grocery store. I was in rebellion to God, which is the sin of witchcraft, or so she said.

Rebekah was so angry at Cheri that day that she took off on her bike to visit her Mexican friend, Eddie, telling him what had just happened. She went for bike rides a lot to think, especially when Cheri made her mad. Eddie told her she was an adult now, and she needed to leave them. He helped her to sneak out that very night.

Another strange occurrence was a time, in the middle of the day, when Rebekah happened to walk inside the camper and see Cheri laughing and talking to the wall in front of her. There was no one else in the room. When Rebekah asked who she was talking to, Cheri said she was talking to angels, holy entities and holy elders. This scared and shocked Rebekah, since there was no one in the room at all. The words that came out of Cheri's mouth sounded like gibberish.

Ruthie and Rebekah decided to leave Cheri alone when she talked to these spirits or entities, even though there was no one physically there in the room. Cheri had been talking to these so-called spirits for quite some time, and this concerned Rebekah.

Cheri had said that these spirits did not want her to go back to the USA or something bad might happen. They would tell her that she could die if she left Mexico. Cheri looked right at Rebekah, before she left the room, and announced, "The spiritual entity in front of me says that we're all to get married." Cheri was to be first, then Ruthie and Rebekah last. It had to be in that order, and if Rebekah got married first, then Cheri was going to die.

Rebekah shook her head as she left the camper, thinking Cheri had been acting strange toward her lately. She was being cold and standoffish, and this was taking it too far.

It was as if she almost sensed Rebekah was going to leave soon. Rebekah thought Cheri was acting a bit too crazy, so she rode her bike over to the home of the pastor of the mission to tell him about everything. He encouraged her to spread her wings and leave Cheri's home.

One last thing Rebekah told me over the phone that bothered her immensely was something else Cheri had told her, shortly before Rebekah left for good. Cheri stated bluntly that she had not married our Dad out of love, like most people, but just for us kids. She wanted to raise us with a *proper* Christian upbringing. The love part had been a scam, a scam against Dad. Rebekah vowed to herself, on the night she left, that she would never return to that environment.

I, too, was shaken upon hearing all of this, and I told Rebekah as I was hanging up the phone, "I will come down to help you as soon as I can get my hands on a plane ticket."

Rebekah thanked me and apologized for not being a good sister all this time. I told her it was not her fault, and I forgave her. Tears were now flowing freely down my face. I said to her, "You didn't have a choice, being enslaved to Cheri playing God!"

Twenty

Stepbrother Adam met Rebekah and her Mexican friend, and took her back to his apartment to stay for as long as she wanted. She was only an hour away from the cabins if she changed her mind and wanted to go back.

I flew down a couple of weeks later. I was overwhelmed with excitement, because for thirty years, I had never really been able to be a big sister to Rebekah.

Rebekah greeted me with a long embrace and showed me her make shift room. Adam had given it to her after his previous tenant moved. The room was spacious with a big bed and writing desk.

She reminded me of myself when I had moved out so many years back, anxious and excited to take on the whole wide world. I felt like we had so much in common. Our looks and mannerisms were almost identical. It was like we were twins with 7 years between us.

Judging Cheri is God's job. But I remember the feeling of being imprisoned by her, with no interaction with other peers my age, and it was not healthy. This caused me to take a long time to adapt in society.

I pondered on the fact that I had had a

sister out there, and for 30 years, we both were not allowed to talk to each other because of the brainwashing and the "religious cult" type of life Cheri was living. This was heartbreaking for me.

I know we all missed out on so much, and now, we have so much catching up to do.

Rebekah got a job after moving in with Adam. Jon helped her get a car. I brought some clothes for her, and she laughed when I gave them to her. She told me one outfit reminded her of the bikini Adam had recently bought her. Adam had taken Rebekah to get a swimsuit at a local store. Rebekah went right over to the plain one-piece suits.

Adam said, "Yuck, there's no way I am going to be caught dead going to the pool with you wearing that."

She put the clothes I brought her in her closet and pulled out her cool new bikini and running shoes Adam had bought for her. She told me, as she showed me her new Nike shoes, she was glad she did not have to hide her exercising anymore. Rebekah told me that if she exercised too much or lost some weight while living with Cheri, Cheri would tell her that she had the "unclean spirit of Blessing" in her.

She liked to take her dog Juno for a walk or jog every day. She thought it was good exercise for the old dog. Upon returning from jogging, she would be in trouble and have to go pray and read her Bible. Cheri made her sign a paper stating she would eat more junk food, soda, and starchy carbohydrates. Rebekah did as she was told, not wanting to be in trouble, and she gained about 200 pounds. She was uncomfortable at this weight and felt sluggish, so she started hiding her exercise and lost some of the weight.

Rebekah and I stayed up late the first night of my visit, and she told me a few hurtful things. One concerned the pictures I had given her after Dad died. Cheri told her they were evil and made Rebekah burn them. I got tears in my eyes at the thought. Cheri had told her that pictures of our Mom were unclean.

It was also bad in Cheri's view when I called on the phone or came to the cabins for a visit. Cheri, in advance, prepared Rebekah by telling her not to answer the phone if I was calling and go to her room or stay away from me as much as possible if I was there.

Rebekah apologized and hugged me as she told me these things. She said she did not mean to ever hurt me or the other siblings when they came to visit. She had been like a puppet with Cheri holding the strings.

I asked her how she felt, now that she knew the truth. She was mad at Cheri. She looked up, as tears were forming in her eyes, and said she did not know what to think or how to feel. She said she knew a lot of what Cheri did, and told her to do, was wrong, but she had been too afraid of getting into trouble to resist.

She had wanted to be independent and make her own decisions, but each time she tried, Cheri stepped in and put a stop to it, saying Rebekah was in rebellion to God and needed to repent.

I told her, the next morning as we went for a jog together, that I was proud of her for moving out and starting a new life that included all her siblings now. She had a blank slate and freedom to make her own choices. I also told her I would always be there to help her as a big sister. I would help her with anything she needed transitioning into society.

I am glad she finally sees the truth about how we were raised. I feel at ease, now that all of us are out of the brainwashed, religious upbringing, and I hope by sharing my story I may inspire others to get out too and be free at last.

Religion is good, and it is terrible. It depends on who is pushing it and how hard it is being pushed. I do not feel like the Bible should be forced down anyone's throat, especially a child's, because they are the most vulnerable. Children are similar to a sponge soaking up water. As a child myself, I was greatly influenced by my parents, thinking everything they said or did was right and true.

Later as an adolescent, I began to question some of the words and decisions Cheri and Dad made. I wondered if God really did speak through them. Why did God never speak to me or my other siblings? It seemed very peculiar and strange.

As an adult, I still believe in God, and I think he can communicate with all of us, not just Cheri, or not just one person in a group.

When younger sister Beth moved out, she told me of a couple bizarre instances that occurred and almost forced her to move out sooner. I implored her to tell me, and it was nearly unbelievable.

According to Cheri, God wanted them to go out in the desert and have a "wilderness experience" and live off the land. God told Cheri they were all to stay in the area and live out in the free range land, because God was going to let them win the lottery. God told Cheri in a vision that they were going to win the power ball jackpot. They had to keep the camper home clean for when the prize patrol came with their lottery winnings.

After a month of not winning, and taking weekly hair washings at a gas station, Cheri announced that one of the siblings was not right with God. She said that was why they did not win the lottery.

They ate prickly pear cactus and jumping cholla plants. Jon and Beth carved utensils out of wood sticks they found in the desert and sold them in town so Cheri and Dad could buy cigarettes. Beth said it was horrible, living out on the desert land, but that was not the clincher.

Cheri decided the brothers and sisters were to marry each other. God had spoken to her in a vision, and Beth was to marry Jon, and Adam was to marry Rebekah.

Beth blew up in Cheri's face and threatened to leave at that very moment. She said there was no way she would marry her brother. It did not matter whether he was her stepbrother or her biological brother, there was no way this could be right, and it could not be what God wanted.

Another insane incident was when everyone went on a field trip to go rock and gem hunting. They were at a dig sight searching when Rebekah announced that she had to go to the bathroom. Cheri said that Rebekah was interrupting their gem search. God divulged that this was a precious gem stone site. Cheri said that Rebekah's sudden outburst of needing to relieve herself had upset God's will for finding this rare, expensive stone. Cheri was furious at Rebekah for this and told her to go and repent.

Beth told me this was awful. Rebekah had glanced a sad look Beth's way and hung her head as Beth obediently walked away to go pray. Instances like this were many in Cheri's household.

Beth also mentioned to Adam about her baby boy being born. She hoped Adam would tell Cheri she was a Grandmother. Adam took the news to his mother, and she took the supposedly grand news terribly, spouting out how the newborn grandson was the devil's child.

Beth cried when she heard this and could not believe how an innocent baby could be deemed the devil's child. I shook my head in disbelief. I was shocked that Beth's own mother, Cheri, could say such an awful thing. I was disgusted.

I did not want to hear anymore. This was becoming too depressing and that was not the point of our conversation. I needed to cheer her up. I told her that I understood why she had left, and I was elated that she was out.

I did not mature as an adult should. Oddly, I seemed childish at age nineteen. I acted more like a sixteen year old because I had no peers my age to socially interact with.

I understand why Dad homeschooled me. He wanted to keep me away from all the peer pressures that teenagers go through: the partying, the drinking, the drugs and sex. I am thankful he kept me safe from these bad influences. I just wish I had a few friends to mature with as I grew into adulthood.

I would still have to deal with peer pressure in society, sooner or later. My Dad did warn me how hard life was going to be out in the real world. I was not prepared and had to learn everything the hard way. Looking back, I try to remember the good things and apply them to life now, and there were some good things to be gleaned from the past.

I was raised on my parents' beliefs about

Biblical rules, but it did not provide me with enough social contact to be normal in society. I missed out on a simple childhood. I lost my Mom at a young age and was controlled and belittled by her replacement. I had no self-esteem when I finally managed to move out on my own. I had literally been degraded until I felt worthless.

I had to learn to love myself. I feel happy with the simple religion and faith that I now have. I have grown and matured in so many ways, and I have adapted to the normal life that I always wanted. My husband loves me and is my best friend. I lead a fulfilling life now, and I am finally proud and thankful in so many ways. Each day is a gift from God, and in fact, it is a Blessing!

About the Author

Blessing Macho lives in Palo, Iowa with her husband and their two Chihuahuas. She enjoys working out at the gym and won a natural bodybuilding contest in 2007. She also enjoys traveling and visiting with family.

Made in the USA
Monee, IL
28 January 2020